What Games Mean

What Games Mean: Understanding Games as Art relates games to established artforms through painting movements, auteur theory, music albums, and documentary. Each chapter discusses the history of the art movement in question and then reads games through those lenses. By defamiliarizing games by thinking about them with atypical genre and form, *What Games Mean* helps create a common language between tabletop and video games and other kinds of art.

This book is about enjoying games in different dimensions as well as offering strategies for game makers to think about their own work and process. Professionals and students can look at games from different perspectives and gain new approaches to how they work.

All this is done considering the roles and responsibilities of artists. These ethical questions are considered in relation to 20th-century art and how it relates to advertisement and propaganda, labor movements and workers' rights in games industries, and how game makers can best interact with their audiences.

Brandon L. Sichling makes games, books, comics, and movies and teaches game design at Northeastern University in Boston. Their work focuses on gender and generational trauma (they are great at parties). Most of their work can be found at brandonlsichling.itch.io, and they have a poem in the upcoming *Pieces of Salem* collection.

What Games Mean
Understanding Games as Art

Brandon L. Sichling

CRC Press
Taylor & Francis Group
Boca Raton London New York

CRC Press is an imprint of the
Taylor & Francis Group, an **informa** business

Designed cover image: Lidia Núñez

First edition published 2027
by CRC Press
2385 NW Executive Center Drive, Suite 320, Boca Raton FL 33431

and by CRC Press
4 Park Square, Milton Park, Abingdon, Oxon, OX14 4RN

CRC Press is an imprint of Taylor & Francis Group, LLC

ISBN: 9781041277408 (hbk)
ISBN: 9781041277392 (pbk)
ISBN: 9781003755821 (ebk)

DOI: 10.1201/9781003755821

Typeset in Minion
by KnowledgeWorks Global Ltd.

Dedication

For everyone who played Super Nintendo with me.

Contents

Acknowledgments

I would like to thank my friends and colleagues Chris Barney, Carly Dwyer, Sam Liberty, Alexandra To, and Fox Zarow for their support and brilliance. I would also like to thank the Cheese Dudes, Jocelyn Geddie, and Neil Jones for their time and thoughtfulness. Thanks to Rekka Alexiel at Fire Sanctuary for your documentation work.

Finally, I'd like to thank my students, past and present. You and your work dazzle me.

Preface: Close Playing

"GENRE" IS A FUNNY word, not least of which because it's one that kids who read are likely to know it by sight and not by sound. I thought it was "jen-rah" and it was words on bookstore shelves and the spines of video cassette boxes. As a form of taxonomy, it's largely useless. Scouring the video store shelves for my favorite characters, I couldn't understand why *Superman: The Movie* was "science fiction" while *Batman* was "action." Why was *Raiders of the Lost Ark* labeled "adventure" and not "war"? As long as people organize and search for art in physical space, genre will be at least as functional as it is theoretical, even if both aspects are mostly intuitive.

Categorizing art is really about describing constellations of audience expectations. As a little kid, I would go to the library and look for *Star Wars* books. I woefully knew I wouldn't find them in "non-fiction," but they weren't in "fiction" either. *Star Wars* opens with a modified "Once Upon a Time…" but it wasn't with other fairy tales. No, *Star Wars* books' spines had stickers with a flying saucer. In fairness, someone browsing the stacks could scan shelves with hundreds of books and easily pick out which were going to be about people doing stuff in space. Same goes for fans of mysteries searching for stickers of a man with a mustache, pipe, and deer stalker cap. If what someone wants is what they expect from a genre, those sticks call out like a drug dealer. "Hey, you lookin' for a locked room mystery?"

Music fans, like people who play games, use genre to self-identify. This often makes people insufferable. In 2025 I encountered, on more than one occasion, the question of what separates pop punk from emo. I thought I left that concern behind in 2006 along with "Jesus is my Homeboy" t-shirts, but alas. Music genre adherence proclaims cultural values and shibboleths. For instance, the difference between "real" punk and pop punk is that the former has a political dimension. "But what about *American Idiot*?" you might ask. "That's definitely pop punk and political." That's correct, but I could say, "That's the exception that proves the rule." Hooray for "no true Scotsman" fallacies.

For games, identification probably has its highest order of taxonomy at whether or not one is a real, capital-G gamer or a (filthy) casual. First-person shooters and fighting games—shooters are about gun fights, and fighting games are about fistfights—are for real, serious gamers. Games for "casual gamers" are whatever genres "hardcore" gamers don't like. While I don't want to dignify nerd elitism by comparing it to anything more deeply historical, this ranking is similar to the history of painting in Europe. Traditionally, real artworks were paintings of high-minded subjects (e.g., scenes from history or mythology, portraits) appropriate for men. Women could paint landscapes or make things that had practical uses, like quilts and water vessels. Similarly, real games are games which threaten failure. Fake games are for people with "political identities." Calling some games or game players "real" makes as much sense as saying only some identities are political.

"Casual" makes sense to me when people use it to express what they want out of games, but don't have to describe the games themselves. It's a way to play. Even blockbuster games often have difficulty settings attuned to the player's desired experience. The options are usually something like "story" or "casual" difficulty for people who want to cruise through the game, followed by increasing difficulty settings for those who "want a challenge" or are "familiar with action games." In this thinking, genre is about the nature of the player's experience and not tied to a game's, or gamer's, worthiness.

Even with a use, "casual" and "hardcore" don't really describe what games actually are. In the early days of *World of Warcraft*, there were think pieces on whether *WoW* was more of a game or a social media platform. Of course, it's both, but the corkboard at your local library is also a social media platform, so maybe that isn't very useful. This was just before Valve's *The Orange Box* was released, introducing the world to *Portal* and its subsequent memes. In the short time "the cake is a lie" was funny, people were asked whether *Portal* was a puzzle game or a first-person shooter. Certainly, it's a puzzle game wherein you solve puzzles using portals. Which you fire. Out of a gun. Sometimes, robots fire guns at you. You know, kind of like that other game with lots of puzzles and sometimes guns, *Resident Evil 4*.

I wouldn't say delineations based on game mechanics have gotten much better in the ensuing years. The PlayStation Store lists games like *Street Fighter 6* and *Teenage Mutant Ninja Turtles: Shredder's Revenge* as "fighting games," despite the former being about 1-on-1 martial arts duels and the latter following four radical teens as they walk screen right and destroy anyone who gets in their way. Both games are about characters who fight, but plenty of people would be hard pressed to name five playable characters who don't fight in one way or another. 1997's *Castlevania: Symphony of the Night* was an adventure game with "RPG (roleplaying game) elements" similar to *Dungeons & Dragons*. *Castlevania* also has dragons, but stats and dragons do not a roleplaying game make. The "roleplaying" is powering up a character rather than making choices which develop the game's plot and characterize an avatar. Now, skill trees are standard enough that people don't bother saying "RPG elements." The current *genre du jour* is "roguelike" or "-lite," which means "you die and lose everything or maybe not everything and there's some randomness in there." You could maybe even describe the accumulation of weapons and power-ups as "RPG elements," but you'd be wrong. Or not.

My concern is that this muddiness in language harms the field in a couple of ways. For one, it's exclusionary. Imagine wanting to start reading superhero comics because you enjoyed a movie about a character. Great. You go into a comic book shop and ask about series with that character and where to start reading. "There's a few," says our hypothetical comic peddler. "This one is an action series with some manga-style page layout and this other one, set in a separate continuity, is more of a Kirbylike" (Different Kirby). It's worse than nonsense because you would feel like you knew what these words meant and glean no useful information.

The other problem is that it limits us in how we think about games, therefore limiting the games we make. A tabletop roleplaying game I really like is Alex Roberts' *Star Crossed*. Its website on Bully Pulpit Games describes it as "a two-player game about really, really wanting to, when you really, really can't." It's about looooove and you know it's smart because the title is a Shakespeare reference. *Star Crossed* players describe what their characters do in relation to scene prompts. Whenever they take a meaningful action, they pull a brick from a tower. If the tower falls over, the responsible player's character confesses their love, actions are tallied, and an ending is decided upon.

It's a lot of fun and, while it has a great tagline, there isn't a cleanly named game genre for it. Romantic video games tend to be dating sims, and they're mostly about guessing what a girl wants to hear and picking that dialog option. Notable exceptions include *Dream Daddy* (pretty much what it sounds like) and *Hatoful Boyfriend* (players date pigeons), but in general video games' romantic relationships are the B-plots of other kinds of stories. In tabletop, romance is usually abstracted as a seduction check or something else done by the numbers. That isn't to suggest *D&D* should call for roleplaying these kinds of scenes. Otherwise, people might be expected to play out *D&D* sex scenes with their friends. And hey, there's nothing wrong with that, but it's also not everyone's thing.

We have the wherewithal to talk about all kinds games, no matter how weird: games are generally suffering from sameyness (a word that is in the Oxford English Dictionary). Mainstream games are so expensive to make that each needs to go for every target demographic. There's every reason not to take a risk when a team has to be all-in to make one multimillion-dollar game every six or so years. Genre currently amounts to people making a handful of types of games and each studio vying to make the best of those types. If we spoke and thought more expansively about games, and bought a wider variety of what is available now, we could have a healthier industry. Putting all the eggs in the "violent man who could use a shave" basket has turned what should be tentpole properties into financial bubbles. It doesn't help job security, that's for sure.

That's all product and marketing stuff, which admittedly I'm less interested in. I'm more interested in how we would play and make games if we valued them the ways we value other artforms. There could be more room for games which say something interesting and do so succinctly. We could have more useful conversations about what makes a game work or not without the debate devolving into a shouting match. Not every game should be a treatise on the human condition or the nature of entropy; some are going to be goofy because that's valuable and good. In no medium should all the texts be one thing or the other because audiences have so much to gain from variety. Better conversations are one way to make the most of those gains.

That might sound like an academic justifying their shouting in the wilderness, and maybe it is, but I also make games and find there are practical reasons to use theory. For one, whatever someone thinks art is, the term is meant to confer some importance. Thinking well about our craft reminds us that we have some kind of responsibility and the work is too important to take seriously. My friend and fellow game designer Sam Liberty, who appreciates the importance of our ethical obligation, is fond of saying, "What we do isn't brain surgery. If we screw up and make a bad game, no one's going to die." True and wise, but games can do harm the way any medium can. We should understand what we want to create, why we want to create that in particular, and how we can best control how that exists in the world. Working as ethically as we can begins by understanding our context and making games that do what we want them to do. Or, at least, make games that get pretty close to that.

I know that studying theory and history has helped me think more deeply about the world around me. I've given some thought as to how that can inform making interesting games, though criticism and theory don't exist to "solve" history. They exist to remind us how humans create, how we affect one another through systems of power, and what it means to speak in response. It behooves anyone who does cultural labor to ask if what we do is worthwhile, and this study has helped me enjoy doing the work.

Thinking about what our world is and how it came to be helps me have, and hopefully expand, my perspective. I believe that helps me share my work with people, and for them to enjoy it. We're social creatures, and all this *thinking* can help us to remember that other people actually exist. Too many people don't act that way, but it's true and a lot of folks are actually pretty great. We should engage with our audiences in ways that respect their time and intelligence, and we might as well benefit from the proven strategies and fascinating missteps of people who have thought well about art. That's the best way, I think, for us to get some respect.

BIBLIOGRAPHY

Sirani, Jordan. "The 10 Best-Selling Video Games of All Time." *IGN*, 18 Feb. 2025, www.ign.com/articles/best-selling-video-games-of-all-time-grand-theft-auto-minecraft-tetris.

CHAPTER 1

The Line Must Be Drawn Here

What Is "Art"?

That depends on who you ask. If you were to ask Pablo Picasso around the time he painted *Guernica*, his depiction of Nazis brutally bombing a town by the same name, he'd say, "Painting is not made to decorate apartments. It's an offensive and defensive weapon against the enemy" (Picasso.org). If you were to ask Chris Pratt, he'd likely get AI's opinion first: "I think you're supposed to say, 'Hey Meta,' like, 'Hey Meta, who eats art?" (Meta)

I'll level with you: anyone who tells you they know what art is, is lying. Maybe I'm projecting. I've confidently declared a definition for art and felt my conscience pang. At those times, I felt as though I had to say *something*. The last time I remember making the argument that something *was* art was in my second semester undergraduate English class. I was arguing video games are art. Since then, I'm pretty sure I've used definitions of art exclusively to exclude works that I wanted not to be considered art. Some of these arguments were well thought out, some were not, but you don't need to be good at geography to find a hill to die on. What I can tell you is I'm reasonably convinced that some games are popular or fine art and many are not. This is much the way some meals are culinary art, but I wouldn't classify peanut butter and jelly sandwiches as such, even if there's a sprig of rosemary on the plate.

DOI: 10.1201/9781003755821-1

My friends, colleagues, and students have offered me many definitions of art, but usually I find them as unsatisfying as I do my own. Hopefully, we can make some progress with a sort of gravitational lensing; if we see how definitions and descriptions of art fail, we should get a better sense of its aspects. I say "sense" instead of "knowledge" because deciding we have an Ultimate Definition of Art would limit how we make, think about, and enjoy art. The opposite of faith is certainty, not doubt. I'm warning you, reader, off the kind of certainty under and for which I labored.

There is the idea that what elevates a thing into Art is that the creator expresses themselves through it. It probably drives people nuts when I retort, "You assume there is a self to express." The self-expression definition fails to account for processes of self-abnegation. Automatic writing, whirling dervishes, Buddhist paintings, and I'd say anything made by an artist sufficiently high would preclude the self to express. The novelist Anne Tyler said of her books, "Pretty soon it's going to be just full of lots of people I've made up. None of the people I write about are people I know. That would be no fun. And it would be very boring to write about me. Even if I led an exciting life, why live it again on paper? I want to live other lives" (Michaels). I think that's something most gamers can relate to, but I think what we do is more akin to imagining living other lives.

I am of the opinion that when we make something, we can't help but encounter ourselves in it and reveal ourselves through it. We also create ourselves when we do anything of substance, so the act of making a game changes the self the game is supposed to express. I'm indulging in metaphysics, but there is something useful here for people who want to make games that sell: it's easier to make interesting games when you have interests. It's true! One's interests don't need to be something other than games. Plenty of wonderful artists have made work reflexive of their medium. Emma Tomblin Marca's *Whale* is a pop-up book version of *Moby Dick* that points out its own artificiality, representing the novel's bizarre story in a format usually for children. I look at *Whale* and think about books more generally. Aren't all books "storybooks"? Should more "serious fiction" embrace multimedia? What if I don't want to call you "Ishmael"? The last isn't general, but *Whale* gets me thinking much the same way a game like *Death Stranding* invites players to reflect. In *Death Stranding*, players take on the role of Normal Reedus and his role in the game (it's weird) of a delivery worker. Players' games are networked and populated with infrastructure other players have built in their own worlds. *Death Stranding* points out that all games create opportunities for us to talk about our play experiences and color one another's memories with those stories.

Naturally, interests outside of games do a lot to enrich the games we make. I had a student who told me they were thinking about switching their major to games. "What's your major now?" I asked. "Neuroscience," they said. I told them not to switch their major and suggested they pick up a games minor instead. There are a lot of games about mental health or set in characters' mindscapes, but I can't think of any games built around how the brain actually works. Someone trained in the field could make a game about any number of...brain...things. My guess is that it would be really helpful in guiding the game design process. If nothing else, advertising real science chops would be a great way for a game to stand out in a storefront. Having interests goes a long way toward having an interesting self to express. It's safe enough to assume there's a self to express.

For someone making a game, the work can communicate the designer not just to the audience, but to the designer themselves. I encourage my own students to look at their games as a way of asking what they really think and feel, because otherwise we lapse into design-by-assumption. It's easy for people to default to assumptions if they aren't all that familiar with a medium, or if they're very familiar with it. If people don't know games very well, they'll remake what they think games are like because that's what they're like (e.g. "board games are about rolling dice and racing to the end of a map"). These non-choices intermingle with other unexamined opinions. For instance, if players are in conflict with each other instead of cooperating against the game system because "that's just what games are," the designer is unintentionally saying the same about human nature.

Overfamiliarity is basically the same trap. Many of my students have grown up playing video games, so I consistently bump into biases about what games "should" have and do. Collectibles and currencies, win- and fail states, limited lives or chances, and randomization are just a few of the things that show up in early versions of games because they're things games just have. This strategy is getting less applicable all the time, but I like to tell designers to imagine what questions their grandparents would ask about a game. "What do the points do?" and "Why are they coins if you can't spend them?" are really good questions for which *Super Mario Bros.* doesn't have answers. I know these kinds of questions help me take a step back and ask if my games have anything more interesting or imaginative to say.

Considering every single decision doesn't make something art. That's not to say it wouldn't be worth doing: that kind of thoughtfulness would almost certainly make it a better game. If the game still winds up bad, obsessive attention to detail can make for a fascinating train wreck. Intentionality is the basis for making anything of quality, and game designers do that in many of the same ways craftspeople and artists have done for approximately forever (Figure 1.1).

FIGURE 1.1 Tompkins Harrison Matteson, Trial of George Jacobs, Sr. for Witchcraft, 1855. Oil on canvas.

Lately, I've been thinking a lot about Tompkins Harrison Matteson's painting, "Trial of George Jacobs, Sr. for Witchcraft, 1855." (That's the year it was painted. The US wasn't still executing people for witchcraft.) Each subject's attention is rapt on someone, directing the viewer's own attention between the fore-, mid-, and background. A lot of figures are pointing, which strengthens the effect. The painting feels frenetic as your eyes dart around to follow the proceedings which led to George Jacobs Sr.'s death by hanging. It's not so very different to how games draw our attention to points of interest by using their skylines, or how they fill us with wonder when a cave opens up on a magnificent cliffside view. Whether or not someone considers any given title to be art, it's outstanding craft and intentional design. The same can be said of a good can opener. I promise you I'm not being flippant. A badly made can opener is a great way to cut yourself trying to get some crushed tomatoes.

Roger Ebert argued that video games (and, I assume, tabletop games) could never be art because players interact with the maker's intentions. Ebert was the most important critic of popular art in his lifetime and certainly one of the most important film critics of all time, but he, by his own admission, should not have publicly weighed in on the question. "I was a fool for mentioning video games in the first place... Some opinions are best kept to yourself" (Ebert). It's a funny thing for him to say considering his career was sharing his opinion and I'm glad he did. I disagree with his argument, but when he said it I had to articulate why. As recently as 2024, Polygon's Patricia Hernandez was still grappling with Ebert's ghost "still haunting the discourse." "The question of whether video games are art should, at this point, feel settled. Instead, the endless comments reveal an uncomfortable truth: All the accolades, the mainstream recognition, and the gargantuan dollar amounts haven't gotten rid of a deep-seated insecurity at the heart of the video game industry" (Hernandez). I see no reason for me not to continue the séance.

In "Okay, kids, play on my lawn," Ebert recounts an exchange he had with film- and game-maker Clive Barker of *Hellraiser* fame. Barker analogized Ebert's contention as, "... Shakespeare could not have written 'Romeo and Juliet' as a game because it could have had a happy ending, you know? If only she hadn't taken the damn poison. If only he'd have gotten there quicker." Barker called on artists to "invent a world where the player gets to go through every emotional journey available." That, he said, was art. "Offering that to people is art."

Ebert responded, "If you can go through 'every emotional journey available,' doesn't that devalue each and every one of them? Art seeks to lead you to an inevitable conclusion, not a smorgasbord [sic] of choices." I'm not sure I agree with "inevitable conclusion." *Ghost of Yotei* has one narrative conclusion. *BioShock* has (basically) two endings, which I'd hardly call a smörgåsbord. That's not even a Lunchables. But "two" is the number of endings available for *Blade Runner* and *Brazil*. One could quibble that these are director's cuts and constitute different movies, which would have us inspecting a knothole and missing the forest.

If Ebert meant that a work of art guides us to one ultimate reading of the work, then I think a whole lot of paintings, sculpture, and music are out. Despite the straightforward name, the 193 pieces of Hilma af Klimt's *Paintings for the Temple* are not going to leave you with an intellectual or emotional conclusion. The *Paintings* are an amazing exploration of line, shape, color, and space. I think they are deeply meaningful, but they are their own conclusion. They have nowhere to lead you. They are inhabitable. Af Klint's works are as arresting as *Tetris*, and I'd argue that's because they are about the same things.

One of the repudiations against Ebert came, ostensibly, from a 16-year-old named Aaron. Aaron's response hinged on video games making money and that playing one all the way through can take a long time. I've heard these points, or permutations of them, plenty of times. They don't hold water: they're just off topic. Profitability and popularity don't make something art. Yes, people spend a lot of money on games. Hell, *I* spend a lot of money on games. Money doesn't imbue an object with spiritual value. My neighborhood has a lot of fantastic public art celebrating Latina artists and our diversity. No one is getting rich off them.

The profitability argument is related to the "cost efficiency" argument. The thrust is that a movie in the theater is about two hours and tickets cost more all the time. That's without concessions, which are always factored in these conversations. I have to concede, concessions are necessary. Games, on the other hand, can be played for hours and hours. Even with $70 as the current standard price for AAA/blockbuster games, a 100-hour game is an arithmetically good return on investment. Granted, between subscriptions and downloadable content (DLC), games can easily cost $90+, but that's for high-production-value titles. Excellent indie games are often $20 or less. I've never heard anyone use the dollar-to-hour argument to compare novels and games.

The cost/benefit ratio doesn't address the argument at hand and is a cynical way to look at entertainment. It reduces cultural works and artifacts by price tagging them like a grocery store. You know, the tag that lists the price of a bag of cheese puffs and its cost per pound. Putting artfulness aside, I've played hundreds of hours of the original *Final Fantasy VII*. I've probably spent less than $50 on it between all the platforms where I've bought it. In 2013, I spent 85 minutes playing the lyrical video game *Dear*

Esther after paying maybe $10. To indulge the medium comparison, I've watched Lynne Ramsay's *Ratcatcher* twice for a grand total of 3 hours and 4 minutes. I bought the Blu-ray on sale for $25. All these titles mean a lot to me, I think about them often, and I'm amazed by each story's power. I can't relate that power with something like a gas pump gauge.

The economic arguments for games being art present evidence (money spent) as a conclusion (this is art). What people are really saying is that games mean a lot to people, so they must be art. I couldn't say if this is an attempt to appear unbiased by using numbers and not feelings or an anxiety around emotions. Either way, if any given work resonates deeply with people, no matter how many or which people, then that thing is probably art.

Whether it makes any money at all, making art is labor. It's a job. Socially, we have this idea that there was some halcyon era of *ars gratia artis* when masters strode the planet revealing truth and beauty. The purest of these were tortured geniuses who died penniless and their work found posthumous profit. These can be moving, but they're historical fictions. Poverty sucks and making money doesn't disqualify a piece from being art.

It's possible, though, that something can be mercenary enough not to be art. A student once asked, "How could something made of art not be art?" It's a good question; I wouldn't tell a concept artist their title is a misnomer. For the students' consideration, I offered the Super Nintendo game *Cool Spot* (Bartz-Todd). "Cool Spot" is the name of the dot in the 7-Up logo, at least when it has arms and legs and wears sunglasses, and in 1993 it got its own multi-platform video game! What a weird time to have been alive!

Cool Spot had a background artist, a composer, animators, and programmers. Certainly, they all worked hard to make the game, especially coaxing The Surfaris' song "Wipe Out" from the lackluster sound systems. It was a pretty good game, at least I remember enjoying it, and it was an advertisement. Whatever we might think of "art" as a social construct, we could agree that a video game made to sell a soft drink is not it. I'd also extend this to games built to facilitate microtransactions. The student who raised the initial question put it, "I guess a game can be less than the sum of its parts."

How much credence we give a game that's also a store or a slot machine is an important question. The ethics are fraught, but I'm more concerned about what it means to put play in a commercial. It's not just a question of games such as *Fortnite* or *Marvel Rivals*, whose business plan sounds like how my generation was warned about people offering us hard drugs ("Hey, kid. The first one's free."). My concern is cultural artifacts manipulating behavior rather than influencing it. We should give less deference to games that are actually stores. People should make games compelling, not imperative. The best comparison for art-as-product, of course, is a theoretical take on post-Renaissance European paintings. Obviously.

"All publicity works upon anxiety. The sum of everything is money, to get money is to overcome anxiety," says John Berger in describing the underlying belief of all advertisements (143). "Oil painting, before it was anything else, was a celebration of private property. As an art-form it derived from the principle that *you are what you have*" (139, original emphasis). But with video games, players often don't possess an object even as it bestows cultural capital. In many video games, real money and/or time can be traded for purely cosmetic outfits—these are called "skins," which is pretty grotesque when you think about it—or any number of facets that may or may not affect the rules. Tabletop games have the same kind of status symbol in crowdfunding backer rewards like stickers or custom dice. These are all for other people to see and create envy, first for the viewer in relation to an imagined version of themself and then envy of the viewer's peers (Berger 132).

"Being envied is a solitary form of reassurance. It depends precisely upon not sharing your experience with those who envy you. You are observed with interest but you do not observe with interest—if you do, you will become less enviable" (Berger 133). That is, not caring that you're envied is cool. "It is a mistake to think of publicity supplanting the visual art of post-Renaissance Europe; it is the last moribund form of that art," since those paintings' concerns are materialistic (Berger 139). These paintings are themselves material to be bought, traded, plundered, sealed away. They cataloged fruit, horses, whatever a noble had to inspire jealousy. Now, I enjoy a multiplayer samurai video game where my time and effort (not money) have bestowed on my sword the ability to make pretty rainbows. Same same, honestly.

While Berger has (plenty of) problems with these paintings, he doesn't deny that they're art. The difference is that the paintings were of things the owner already had and solidified his view of himself. Commercials make people dissatisfied with themselves, not with the way society is structured (142). You aren't lonely and stressed because you spend 40+ hours a week at a job that doesn't pay you enough to live comfortably. You're lonely and stressed because you haven't bought the kitchen implements from Amazon to cook a meal you can post to Instagram so other people can be jealous. Some of the symbols of cultural capital in games function similarly: a deluxe edition of a tabletop game is an actual object. A statue that comes with a pre-ordered video game actually exists. But I cannot abide the idea that a game is art if it was made to sell more and more of itself. A Skinner box isn't art.

If I had to commit to a definition, and I've been putting that off long enough, I'd say an artwork is something designed to guide audiences through an emotional experience of being human. Artists have to make decisions about accessibility and perspective, which is why I'm going with "designed." I think it needs to be an emotional experience because an intellectual experience is a proof. I am not sure what it means to *be* human, but I'm doing my best. My definition excludes a lot of wonderful things and includes things the world would be better without. Art is important, but it's not something to fetishize. It's simply a thing people do. It can be a job or a hobby. Whether or not art is necessary, life is better with it.

Some of what fits my definition is tedious. I don't want to exclude bad art from my definition; some jokes aren't funny, but they're still jokes.

Sometimes, we think art is necessarily life-affirming, but some awful people have made harmful art. John Wayne Gacy painted clowns. Well, he made paintings *of* clowns. Leni Riefenstahl made films to "celebrate the rebirth of the body and of community," as long as that community was of Nazis (Sontag 86). The point is, I'm including artworks we would rather not exist at all. My definition, and its permissiveness, likely doesn't match people's assumptions of art. In my experience, people feel about art the way they feel about reading.

I remember the beginning of *Harry Potter* as a global phenomenon. People, both for and against, lost their minds over it. Putting aside the more extreme accusations—that *Harry Potter* taught children how to do literal witchcraft—there was a general understanding that these were children's books and deserved derision or defense. "Sure, it's a kids' book," said exasperated people with a handle on reality, "but at least it got kids reading." It felt like a bunch of adults who didn't eat vegetables admitting that, yes, the cheese product is bad for the children, but there's broccoli in there.

On balance, yes, vegetables are good for you (and cheese is wonderful), but it's not as if all reading is equal and beneficial: *Atlas Shrugged* is a book. In "Staying Awake," Ursula K. LeGuin cites a National Endowment of the Arts survey, "To Read or Not to Read," which "lamented the decline of reading, warning that non-readers do less well in the job market and are less useful citizens in general." LeGuin was unfazed. "It's just that not all that many people ever did read [books]. Why should we think everybody ought to now?" (Matter 37). She observed that in 1850-1950 reading and having a broad base of knowledge bestowed cultural cache. Engaging with the arts continues to grant one more social worth.

The implication is that "undesirable" people are merely entertained by, say, watching a video of someone falling off a roof but not getting hurt very badly. As of this writing, *America's Funniest Home Videos* is still on the air. This idea really is just classism. The obscenely rich are capable of watching Bong Joon Ho's *Parasite* and thinking it's a real neat movie. Working people can see the broader social implications of injuring a man's genitals in the short film "Man Getting Hit by Football" (A Star Is Burns).

The division between "fine" and "pop(ular)" art is hazy. The line between "art" and "entertainment" is porous. Fine art usually means "something you find in a museum." It has great cultural worth. If you understand it, you must be smart. It would look at home in a rich person's house. The most important thing is that it fits into a history of how we (are meant to) understand art. Traditionally, fine art is Renaissance-style work celebrating the nude human form (think *Birth of Venus*). That type of subject was valued over "decorative" subjects like still life and landscapes

> In the field of art history, the white Western male viewpoint, unconsciously accepted as the viewpoint of the art historian, may–and does–prove to be inadequate not merely on moral and ethical grounds, or because it is elitist, but on purely intellectual ones. In revealing the failure of much academic art history, and a great deal of history in general, to take account of the unacknowledged value system, the very presence of an intruding subject in historical investigation, the feminist critique at the same time lays bare its conceptual smugness, its meta-historical naivete.
>
> (*NOCHLIN 1*)

The field of fine art still struggles to connect with broader audiences because those of us from the working classes perceive or imagine that "conceptual smugness." Or, as Berger put it, "The majority take it as axiomatic that the museums are full of holly relics which refer to a mystery which excludes them: the mystery of unaccountable wealth" (24). Even if the painting or what-have-you in question is "pop" art (not to be confused with "popular art"), working people are assumed not to "get it." A great example is *The Simpsons* season 10 episode 19: "Mom and Pop Art." If you feel like you should recognize that but don't want to look it up: "Le grille? What the hell is le grille?"

In the episode, Homer fails to assemble "le grille." The result is mistaken (recognized?) as a powerful piece of "outsider art," which is about as condescending a term as you can get. Homer needs inspiration, Marge takes him to the museum, and the joke is that Homer sounds like an idiot appreciating it. Two things. First, Marge knows a *lot* about the pieces on display, which are from disparate schools of thought and media. Secondly, art is allowed just to be neat. I mean, sure, it can add a lot to the enjoyment of an artwork if you know a bit about its story and context, but worrying about "getting" a painting is the best way not to enjoy it.

"Popular" art produced for a larger audience, whether or not it's actually popular. Mainstream, as opposed to experimental, movies are a good example of the "Fine > Popular" hierarchy because they are assumed to be for less discriminating audiences. What interests me about popular art is how we vaguely rank its validity. Every so often when I'm talking movies, someone will guiltily tell me they "don't know much about film." If I argue their opinion is just as worthy as mine, they'll use my film degree against me (how dare they). Suffice to say there is a wide range of knowledge among film degree holders.

People who "don't know much about games," though, say it as a matter of fact. The apology I detect on those occasions is to me for them not getting what I do. They're not worried about sounding uncultured. And they shouldn't be. For the record, I don't begrudge anyone for not playing games. I begrudge them for not playing *my* games.

Few games fit the traditional fine art model, but a lot sit pretty comfortably at the popular art table. It's worth mentioning that even respectable museums have integrated games into their collections. The Museum of the Moving Image has rotating exhibitions of niche video games as part of their larger effort to "connect diverse communities to the moving image, in all its forms, with the goal of together building a more equitable and inclusive future" (Moving Image). Even New York City's Museum of Modern Art has made space for games. Their 2003 exhibition *Never Alone* contained historically important titles (e.g., *Pac-Man* and *Minecraft*) alongside headier, more sophisticated games. One was the eponymous *Never Alone*, a game based on an Iñupiat folktale and made in collaboration with the Cook Inlet Tribal Council. Another was *Getting Over It with Bennett Foddy*, a game in which players take on the role of Diogenes and use a hammer to claw their way up a mountain of junk (*Never Alone*).

There is a sense that art, or *real* art, is demanding, unpleasant, or boring. If you're enjoying yourself, it can't be good for you. As most games at least want to be fun, people have the understandable tendency to regard them as toys. People who remember the early 90s might recall Nintendo displays at Toys "R" Us and KB Toys. Department stores shelved tabletop games like *13 Dead End Drive* and *Mouse Trap* next to action figures and LEGO sets. *Dungeons & Dragons* is played with figurines. An especially violent game constitutes a tasteless cartoon for grown-ups.

Never Alone and *Getting Over It* are such good examples of art because while they are intentionally designed games, there's something more to them. *Never Alone,* or *Kisima Innjitchuŋa* in Iñupiat, casts players as Nuna, an Iñupiat girl, and her Arctic fox as they save her village from a relentless blizzard (Vesce, Hope). It's a fun and beautiful game that shares core elements with *Super Mario,* but *Never Alone* is a documentary both in its gameplay and its short films on the Iñupiat way of life. It's a fantastic exploration of culture.

Getting Over It with Bennett Foddy, on the other hand, must be art because I cannot imagine a more miserable game. That's what its fans like about it. That's what those sickos *want.* As Chris Plante put it in Polygon's "The 50 best games of 2017" list, "The player users a sledgehammer to push, pull and pop a bald man in a cauldron up and over a mountain. Ultra difficult games can be demoralizing… But Foddy converses with the player, encouraging them forward."

It's a lovely sentiment, and one I am positive I would not share, but Plante's point stands. It helps that the man in cauldron is named for one of Cynicism's founders. To me, it seems to be the video game equivalent of a Marina Abramović piece. But, as Camus wrote, "The struggle itself towards the heights is enough to fill a man's heart. One must imagine

Sisyphus happy" (89). But we don't have to imagine! As of December 6, 2017, over 2.7 million people have played *Getting Over It*. I'm sure at least a couple of them were happy. Eventually (Wood).

Museums change games' contexts and expand how we think of their meaning. Sure, the game itself is the same on a home PC or in the MoMA, but museums' curation invites players to consider the game's material history. I played a digital version of Hnefatafl, or "Viking Chess," at the Danish National Museum and found myself wondering how useful it was for teaching military tactics and how Vikings might have transported their Hnefatafl sets. I also wondered if I was pronouncing "Hnefatafl" correctly. Probably not.

The rub is, socially and economically speaking, being art isn't what gets a piece in a museum. Being in a museum is what makes something art. If nothing else, museums legitimize work and create further opportunities for exhibition or sales. The more well-known an artist is, the more impressive it is for a collector to own their work and the more a buyer will be willing to pay. This is the case even when the artwork is a joke on the establishment. The classic example is *Fountain*, a urinal submitted by painter Marcel Duchamp under the pseudonym "R. Mutt" and rejected by the Independents art show in New York's Grand Central Palace. Nonetheless, it found its way back into the gallery, *et voilà*, the urinal became art (de la Durantaye).

My favorite piece of "fuck you" fine art is *Love is in the Bin*. There's this great video Banksy made about making it called "Shred the Love." In the video, attendees of Sotheby's London sip champagne and stuff canapés down their gullets. Someone says, with no sense of irony, "That's the nice thing about auctions: everyone's got a chance." A painting adaptation of Banksy's mural *Girl with Balloon* goes for $1.4 million ("Banksy"). As soon as it sells, someone hits a button on a remote. The shredder hidden in the frame activates and turns half the painting into very pretty fettuccine, then jams. Apparently, "in rehearsals it worked every time…" ("In rehearsals") The bummer is that despite the obvious panic on the part of Sotheby's, the destruction became part of the piece's aura. "Banksy didn't destroy an artwork in the auction, he created one… newly titled Love Is in the Bin, the first artwork in history to have been created live during an auction" ("Woman who bought"). In 2021, Sotheby's auctioned *Love is in the Bin* again for £18,582,000, or about $24.7 million ("Banksy Brings down").

One of the things I like about games as a field is that they're not *real* art. In film school, I was told real art has "rules" you have to learn before you "break." That stodginess is what makes something *real ahht*. Naturally, there are no natural rules for making art. It's either interesting or boring, but if people in positions of authority decide there's a right way to do something, they'll discourage experimentation. Our thinking around games doesn't seem to have calcified as much because they're viewed primarily as designed experiences, so whatever works, works.

Maybe, to some extent, a little bit, I worry that releasing a book about games as art will fossilize them. I don't want games to be counterpoints to real art. I want to demolish the idea of real art.

Unlike paintings, sculpture, etc., games don't have originals. Fine art is partly what it is because any copies are copies of a particular piece (Berger 21). An original has a context and an aura that changes as people experience it throughout time (Benjamin 6). Games' auras are not tied to specific, but rather mass produced, objects. Like books and movies, games may have different editions or special releases, but it wouldn't make any sense to say something is the "original" *Sonic the Hedgehog*, unless you meant a copy of the first game in the series. You could have authenticated original concept art or production documentation, maybe one of the computers developers made to build a game, but there's no "master" of a video game. We tend to think of tabletop games as more physical than video games, and they do create artifacts, but they're similarly mass produced.

It might be useful to unpack "master," since a lot of popular games from the last few years have been remasters. In recording media, the master is duplicated for production. If we take music as our example, performances are used to make the master copy, and copies are then made from that master.

Walter Benjamin's "The Work of Art in the Age of Mechanical Reproduction" explores how reproduction changes a work of art's aura, which an original has by virtue of being reproduced. While originals and masters can degrade over time, video games can be reproduced instantly and perfectly with a copy/paste, which can shake some of the burden of aura. The irony here is that older games are often under threat of being lost, since they're tied to the hardware for which they were built, and that gives them a sense of mystery.

This is a bit superficial, but there's something to be said for playing a Super Nintendo game on an original console jacked into a cathode-ray tube TV. In a small way—like an ancient statue of Venus was an "object of veneration" for the Greeks and an "ominous idol" for Middle Ages clerics—an old game played on old hardware has a different meaning for someone playing it today than it did when it was first released (Benjamin 6). Playing on old hardware today could be about nostalgia, skill, or history. Playing it on new hardware (there are lots of new machines to play old games) or computer emulators with quality-of-life tools offers a much more accessible experience.

Physical context is one thing, but Benjamin's point is more important than whether or not I'll ever be able to finish a *Fire Emblem* game from when they were much harder (probably not). His point is political. "The greatly increased mass of participants has produced a change in the mode of participation. The fact that the new mode of participation first appeared in a disreputable form [film] must not confuse the spectator. Yet some people have launched spirited attacks against precisely this superficial aspect" (17). Benjamin quotes Georges Duhamel's *Scènes de la vie future* to illustrate the disdain for film audiences: "[the movie is] a pastime for helots, a diversion for uneducated, wretched, worn-out creatures... a spectacle which requires no concentration and presupposes no intelligence" (17). This sounds enough like how games, video and tabletop role-playing, were talked about in the 80s and 90s.

Benjamin warns readers that applying concepts such as "creativity and genius, eternal value and mystery" to culture and material realities "would lead to a processing of data in the Fascist sense" (2). By way of definition, I'll pull from "Ur-Fascism," in which Umberto Eco described fascism as "a *fuzzy* totalitarianism, a collage of different philosophical and political ideas, a beehive of contradictions" (Original italics). Even so, fascist movements have similar tendencies, including demonizing "degenerate" art and intellectuals, accusing universities of being "a nest of reds" (communists), and squelching disagreement. For "people who feel deprived of a clear social identity, Ur-Fascism says that their only privilege is the most common one, to be born in the same country." In fascism, "there is no struggle for life, but, rather, life is lived for struggle," and people under fascism are meant to see themselves as heroes in a great struggle. Fascists sublimate the "difficult games" of living by "transfer[ing] his will to power to sexual matters." Eco asserts this as the origin of misogyny and homophobia, and a disdain for asexuality: "[s]ince even sex is a difficult game to play, the Ur-Fascist hero tends to play with weapons—doing so becomes an ersatz phallic exercise." For an uncomfortable example of that last one, see how people talk about "Daddy Trump."

It's not hard to find this thinking in games, or at least in too many of their players. Look around on the Internet, and you'll see the dumbest form of solipsist accusing others of being NPC's (non-player characters). Because many games are inspired by fairy tales, they assume the legitimacy of monarchy and follow the power fantasy of the strongest servant, not of the revolutionary. Steve Bannon used Gamergate and gaming-adjacent websites to test his racist, misogynist playbook for getting Donald Trump elected (Warzel). And while it's hard to tell how representative it is, a post on theRPGsite.com's forum warns people against role-playing publishers who are anti-racist or pro-consent (Ocule).

Incidentally, there's a history of right-wing commentators weighing in on art, even if they only care about it enough to whip themselves up into a frenzy. This is maybe my Middle American upbringing, but I heard plenty of people talk about why modern art was bad because artists are "supposed" to provide us with a clear statement. It's not about a feeling or an experience: it's about having an answer. Interesting art does come from a clarity of thought, but people don't always need to know those thoughts to enjoy the work. It's fine that playing along and dealing with uncertainty isn't everyone's cup of tea, but that's not what these arguments are about.

If you're not sure to which episode in history I'm referring, I'll give you a hint: "degenerate art" in Deutsche is "Entartete Kunst" and it eroded "decency and family values" (Wilson). That didn't stop the Third Reich from selling stolen artworks to fund their warmongering, but the will isn't going to triumph without a little spending money (Wilson). As you might expect, this sentiment hasn't gone away. It's gone to Twitter, "where attacking such modernist upstarts as Picasso, Duchamp, and the Impressionists" is a way of protecting Western civilization from degeneracy (Greig).

Writing on the Los Angeles County Museum of Art's 1991 recreation of the degenerate art exhibition, the LA Times' art critic William Wilson observed, "But we have experienced enough ongoing economic uncertainty, military anxiety, minority prejudice, anti-intellectualism and general coerciveness so that the psychological vectors coming out of 'Entartete Kunst' have an eerie resonance." This was around the same time Pat Buchanan attacked President and *Simpsons* guest star George H.W. Bush for funding "blasphemous" and "so called" art which "glorified homosexuality, exploited children, and perverted the image of Jesus Christ" (C-SPAN). The artwork in question was Marlon Riggs' *Tongues Untied*, a funny, angry, and beautiful exploration of being Black and gay in the late 80s and early 90s. Racism and homophobia infect online discourse whenever mainstream modern artists try to do bring about an awful world where people are treated with respect. Gasp. (Watson).

People manipulating games for political ends wouldn't have come as a surprise to Benjamin: "[Humanity's] self-alienation has reached such a degree that it can experience its own destruction as an aesthetic pleasure of the first order. This is the situation of politics which Fascism is rendering aesthetic" (20). If connecting politics and aesthetics seems spurious, the President of the United States is a former game show host, and the Secretary of Education made her fortune through professional wrestling. While *South Park* has never been apolitical, its creators have had to confront politics for the same reason they satirized *World of Warcraft*: "Whether it's the actual government or whether it is all the podcasters and the TikToks and the YouTubes and all of that, and it's just all political and political because it's more than political. It's pop culture" (Ricciardi).

There's been a lot of ink spilled writing screeds about how games should stay out of politics, that games are just for escapism, and critics/critical players should simply focus on the game. Epic Games (of *Fortnite* fame) founder and CEO Tim Sweeney proposes the "separation of church and state" approach for video games. His argument is that the kind of divisiveness that leads to chicken sandwiches being ammunition in culture wars—alluding to backlash to Chik Fil-A funding hate groups—and "that's really dumb" (Kim). Yes, it is dumb that a fast food restaurant and its higher-ups give money so people will be denied rights. But is it really so dumb for people to get angry about that? Isn't it reasonable for Americans to want equal rights for all citizens and for everyone to whom America's laws apply to have equal legal protections? I think that's a perfectly good reason to eat at Popeye's instead.

Games have never been apolitical and they certainly aren't now. For instance, *Fortnite* has crossed over with Disney (*Avengers*, *Star Wars*, *The Simpsons*) and Warner Bros. (*Space Jam*, DC Super Heroes) intellectual properties. The Walt Disney Corporation successfully lobbied to change copyright law, owns ABC News, and censored a kiss between two women in *Star Wars Episode IX: The Rise of Skywalker* for international releases. Working with them is not neutral. It's the same with Warner:

they copyrighted the very idea behind the Nemesis System in which enemies adapt to and remember player interactions. It's a really cool idea, not software, that WB patented. Naturally, they canceled the only game that was going to make use of it post-copyright, and that was a Wonder Woman game (Bonk). That's all kinds of political. I understand wanting to maximize profit; obviously, that's what I'm all about as an independent artist and teacher, but it's wild to say games can exist in this context and be apolitical.

Even more directly, there are myriad games about international armed conflict. Those are, necessarily, political. Even the game's production value contains rhetoric: the better and cooler something looks, the better and cooler its underlying thinking appears. "War is beautiful because it combines the gunfire, the cannonades, the cease-fire, the scents, and the stench of putrefaction into a symphony," Benjamin quotes the Italian Futurists to support his argument that "all efforts to render politics aesthetic culminate in one thing: war" (19). But while *Call of Duty: Modern Warfare* and *Battlefield* revel in "fiery orchids of machine guns," they are not interested in a "symphony" of offal and effluvia. They are interested in portraying the United States and its allies as heroes in a fun representation of war. In fairness, these are primarily multiplayer games and that mode doesn't need to be deeper than Capture the Flag at summer camp. I get that. I also get that portraying real armies and their real weapons as dangerous toys has politics (as would using fictional soldiers and weapons). I don't expect a game about recovering from a gunshot wound at a VA hospital, but how we portray the kind of violence that really happens affects how we think about that violence. And there might be a reality in which a game about painful physical therapy and nerve damage is fun, but it would be a tough sell.

It behooves each of us to recognize that not everyone finds the same topics distasteful, worrisome, or tedious, so a game having a political perspective isn't necessarily bad. It's also true that players can play with politics sometimes and not others. That became real for me when a dungeon master (or "DM," the game runner for *Dungeons & Dragons*) pointed out to me that systemic violence against, and demonization of, unhoused people isn't analogous to orcs. Orcs are not real, so they can just be evil and deserve to die. Fair enough. We do not live in a world like *D&D*'s, and it isn't always useful to impose our social conventions on fictional worlds.

Fire Emblem: Three Houses, set in a military academy for noble children, fairly directly grapples with relevant themes. The students are divided into the houses by country; one is a theocratic empire, and children with "good breeding" are valued more highly than their classmates. That is, some students are the products of arranged marriages meant to cultivate children with magical crest birthmarks. My gut reactions were "if that's not eugenics it's close enough" and "theocracy is inherently evil," and while those positions aren't hard to defend, I gave them a bit more thought anyway.

It's not hard to read the *Three House*'s crests as metaphors for the supposed superiority of people who are born privileged. Similarly, it's a short jump to go from the game's holy empire to any real authoritarian theocracy: gods and their emissaries don't rule by the consent of the governed. The important difference is that wealth and connections are not talent or intelligence, but they can seem that way. *Three House*'s magic is just straight-up real, though, and gives some child soldiers an edge. Similarly, there is no concrete, empirical proof of god(s), but in *FE: Three Houses*, you eventually get weapons MADE OF GODS' BONES. It would be easy for me to write off any of the game's factions as evil because of similarities to real-world governments, but that's just less interesting. It's fascinating to consider the ethics of raising magic child soldiers when the safety of a nation depends on them for martial might. I can wrap my head around a king who doesn't want to piss off a wrathful god. While the politics of *Three Houses* is not our world's politics, we can relate to how these characters act under the stresses of war and high school.

"The aim of all commentary on art now should be to make works of art-and, by analogy, our own experience-more, rather than less, real to us" (Sontag). We get more out of art we engage with as it is, but in the context of our world. People complain that elements like the Pride flags in *Marvel's Spider-Man 2* ruin games because games are meant to be an escape from reality (Pride flags). When someone demands games be apolitical to foster escapism, they're saying what in our reality they want to escape. Sony censored Pride flags from the Saudi Arabian release of *Spider-Man 2* because Sony places profit over their developers' principles. For some people, that is the "better version" of the game, but throwing a temper tantrum over representation isn't about escapism; it's about ignorance (Baculi).

"As for the charge of escapism, what does 'escape' mean? Escape from real life, responsibility, order, duty, piety, is what the charge implies. But nobody, except the most criminally irresponsible or pitifully incompetent, escapes to jail. The direction of escape is toward freedom. So what is 'escapism' an accusation of?" (LeGuin) Ursula K. LeGuin was writing about fantastical literature, but the sentiment fits games nicely. If LeGuin was correct, games, literature, and art in general should give us a chance to think outside of social strictures. Practicing criticism is important because it's a way to explore how art can question "our conventions, our belief, our orthodoxy, our construction of reality" (LeGuin). Things don't have to be this way, and criticism at its best is a tool to expand what people can do with imagination.

This book's purpose is not to put forward a taxonomy of game criticism, nor am I interested in sharing my "correct" reading of the games I discuss. My interest here is to look at art history and criticism, both fine and popular, and relate games to these lenses of experience. In each chapter, I'll pick a concept, or family of concepts, and look at some games through that lens. I don't want to calcify these games and our thinking about them in a "tradition," but I think these are fun ways to talk about what games mean and why they mean so much to us. Plus, talking about a game as being "impressionist" or "lyrical" is at least as useful and intelligible as saying a game is "a metroidvania soulslike with roguelite elements." That sounds more like a diagnosis.

In my time as an artist and arts educator, I've come to believe that it's criticism that even makes something art. I don't mean, exactly, that critics decide what is and isn't art. The Borscht Belt punchline "everyone's a critic" is true. Like cooking and driving, critiquing is a thing a lot of people do. Some people do it professionally. Professional critics influence how we think about art, which in turn influences what we seek out, recommend, and buy. When someone is critical enough about a thing to say something interesting about it, they have also made art.

What real criticism isn't is rules, as in "you have to know the rules before you can break them." I was workshopping a screenplay in which two young women kiss and one of the girls's brother walks in on them. People had a problem with the brother getting a whole line of the script to react. No dialog, just his face.

"It's not his scene," I was told.

"Yes, but he's in the scene."

"But it's not about him."

The correct way to write this scene was to have a character exist only to serve as a threat for the main characters. Whether or not seeing his reaction was interesting was neither here nor there. So I asked, with genuine curiosity, why someone like Jim Jarmusch can make oddball movies, and they're all on the Criterion Collection, but if I try something, people aren't willing to play along.

"He has a whole movie to play with these ideas," my professor said. "When you have only a few minutes, you have to make your point clearly." Now, you tell me how much runway could be enough to understand the story of a hitman in 90s New York who buys ice cream from his francophone best friend before raiding a mob safehouse using the same tactics as a *Looney Tunes* bear? (Whitaker) I don't think there's enough scaffolding for that; you just have to be willing to play along. Criticism should give, or take, the right to value art just because it's interesting.

There are tremendous game critics, professional and amateur, but the field still contends with whether or not a game is a product with a purpose. That's a hell of an assumption right there. Like the object of criticism, critique is either interesting or it's tedious. "Ignore the politics in the game, is the game fun?" is tedious.

Complaining critics have bias is complaining they have a point of view. Review aggregators strike me as odd because they take points of view and turn them into data. The percentage of how many reviews are favorable is more of a buyer's guide than it is a critique. It would be nice if humans curated the most insightful or persuasive critiques, but that isn't computational and "unbiased." Once when I was making this argument, a student asked whether it's a critic's responsibility to represent the opinions of as much of the audience as possible.

It's an interesting question because if the critic tried to preempt consensus, they wouldn't be critiquing. They'd be guessing how they thought something would land with its presumed target audience. Critics do consider for whom a game, movie, et cetera is made and will try to meet it on those terms, but it's a much more interesting question when it cannot be answered. I'm reminded of the first live action *Teenage Mutant Ninja Turtles* movie. In the middle, there's a sequence in which the Turtles and their human friend April O'Neil hide out at a farmhouse in upstate New York while Raphael recovers from the beating of his life. The Turtles and April journal, draw, reflect. The camera lingers as April narrates in the tone you might expect from a Virginia Woolf adaptation if Woolf wrote about mutant turtles in the bloom of their lives. That movie rules, but as a kid I had no idea what was going on in that part, and not every part of every artwork has to be for every audience member all the time.

People argue critics don't create anything, but merely tear down those who take the risk of creation. "It is not the critic who counts; not the man who points out how the strong man stumbles," tweeted *Last of Us* voice actor Troy Baker, quoting Theodore Roosevelt. "…if he fails, at least he fails while daring greatly, so that his place shall never be with those cold and timid souls who neither know victory nor defeat." That sounds heroic, but really it's avoiding the issue. Baker is arguing that, whether or not a piece of criticism is correct, the person who said it doesn't matter and therefore their opinion is worthless.

Oscar Wilde took more or less the opposite position. "The etcher of a picture robs the painting of its fair colours, but shows us by the use of a new material its true colour-quality, its tones and values, and the relations of its masses, and so is, in his way, a critic of it, for the critic is he who exhibits to us a work of art in a form different from that of the work itself" (Wilde 1824). An artist shares a meaningful experience, but a critic has to react meaningfully. While I find agreeing with a critic convenient and aggrandizing, disagreeing is a chance to refine my reasoning and feeling. It's also a good exercise for those of us who make art. I've had instances where my enjoyment, or even engagement, with something was limited by thinking about how *I* would have done it. Then again, liking everything isn't a perspective, or as Wilde put it, "Bad artists always admire each other's work. They call it being large-minded and free from prejudice. But a truly great artist cannot conceive of life being shown, or beauty fashioned, under any conditions other than those that he has selected" (Wilde 1856).

People who make games, and a lot of people who play them, want more depth and breadth in what games are and do. From what I can tell, examining how we want games to exist in the world is the most valuable part of this discussion of games as art and art itself. The expansion I'd like to see is textual, for games to explore more subjects and styles, but it's also technical. Similar to early filmmakers developing editing theory to compress and elongate time and space, game designers can more deliberately pursue techniques for making games. I mention film editing because movies expanded our artistic lexicon. Other media approximate and capitalize on film editing, but it was the material itself that early practitioners manipulated to develop new aesthetics. These ideas then develop within and across art forms. Eventually, as happened with film, the ideas develop enough for someone to call their products "art."

One source of validation for games is reactionaries working themselves into a lather over them. People were worried *Dungeons & Dragons* was going to make their kids into psychotic killers (Lazarus) or devil worshipers who could use magic to take control of their parents (Chick). Way back in 2007, Fox News was very concerned about *Mass Effect*'s full nudity and players' "complete control" over sex scenes. They aired a segment titled "SE'X'BOX?" and Fox's "expert" simply lied about the game. Geoff Keighley represented video games as a whole and defended the game on its artistic merit (Fox).

Even if games are still low art to many people, game makers have every reason to provoke and discomfort. By understanding how our work relates to movements and schools of thought within art, we can build on other artists' work and further develop game aesthetics.

When I say "aesthetics," I don't only mean how they look or sound. As Rosa Menkman says in *The Glitch Studies Manifesto*, "The dominant, continuing search for a noiseless channel has been, and will always be no more than a regrettable, ill-fated dogma" (1). Instead, we can develop games as "a medium in a critical state (a ruined, unwanted, not recognized, accidental and horrendous state)" and make something new of "genre, interface and expectations" (Menkman 8). Or, as music producer Brian Eno put it, "Whatever you now find weird, ugly, uncomfortable and nasty about a new medium will surely become its signature…CD distortion, the jitteriness of digital video, the crap sound of 8-bit—all of these will be cherished and emulated as soon as they can be avoided" (283). And it's true: I know teenagers who like CDs and LPs, I have a fondness for film grain, and despite developers' best efforts to prevent texture warping on old PlayStation games, people love the lo-fi look (Litchfield).

There's no better example of what video games *are* that *Cyberpunk 2077* at launch. It was a mess and it was amazing. My favorite reported glitch is had the player character T-posing (standing with their arms stuck out) while they were driving. Funniest part? No pants.

It was not a great time for the game's studio, CD Projekt Red. Don't worry, they're doing fine, and they fixed *Cyberpunk 2077*. What I'm saying is, maybe it shouldn't have. The native aesthetic of any medium is when it drops, or fumbles, the pretension of perfection. It's seeing brush strokes or washed-out video. By looking at games and their contexts as material, we can develop and expand what they do and mean. For games, that's play itself. A game's animations, music, and so on are all part of its aesthetic, but I'm not interested in making games look like paintings or sound like albums. They've been doing that, and well, for a long time. I'm interested in grappling with how to conceptualize the feelings we get from play itself.

Better understanding play's aesthetics isn't as a way of legitimizing games for people outside our field or making a shibboleth for the in-crowd. Relating how we think and feel while playing games to how we experience other art forms is a way for designers to steal other artists' strategies. My hope is to enrich both work and play.

Good artists create. Great artists exploit glitches.

In August of 2013, Jef Aldrich and Jon Taylor started a podcast with the "aim to dig deep in the used shelves and bargain bins of gaming stores across the country and bring you up-to-the-minute reviews of long-dead roleplaying games" (System Mastery). Since then, *System Mastery* has released over 300 episodes and expanded to reviewing movies, TV shows, and *Star Wars* novels. They've also written the *Düngeonmeister* series of RPG-themed cookbooks, trivia books, and there's even a coloring book in there.

B: When you started *System Mastery*, it played like a podcast for reviewing bad movies, but for roleplaying games. How has that changed over the past 12 years and what's stayed the same? How would you describe the ways your critique has changed?

Jon: Definitely when we started out, I think we aired a little more on the side of comedy than strict review. I think a lot of that ended up being a little more comedically angry at games.

Jef: Yeah, I think we were doing a little bit more of an Angry Video Game Nerd thing. We were hyperbolically playing up the anger in the early years.

Jon: But even then, I think there was a bit starting out when you do dive into the like really the deep end of sort of bad games and you have for the most part been like… You know, I've played probably more than the average person who has played maybe a couple editions of *D&D*, but once you really go into that, you go, oh, wow, this is not good.

It can be very like jarring to see just the depths of that. But I do think as the years have gone on, and we've done this for over a decade now, there is a familiarity with it. I think breeds a level of not, I wouldn't say, complacency, but just a level where you go, "Oh, I understand now that this is not something that was a weird offshoot, oh, this person was insane for doing these things." You're like, oh, this was a trend. It wasn't so much that this person was bad at designing. That was just sort of what was being done at the time. And when you see something where you go, oh, they were trying to break out. They were trying to do something new. And when you look at it from a modern perspective: "Oh, that didn't work at all."

How could [those designers] not have known this would be awful? But, you know, back then all anyone knew was, you know, rolling 3d6 and having strength and dexterity and that was it. They would say, "We're going to do this new system and try to make some brand new thing."

And it doesn't work at all, at least nowadays when I'm looking at a game like that, as opposed to back then I go, well, you were trying something. Bless you for even doing that.

Jef: One of the things that we've started to say about the games is even at their worst, even the games that are abhorrent or poorly thought out or everything's spelled wrong in them, they got that thing published.

Yeah, there's a level of respect I have to put on people who take their vision and get it all the way to the finish line, even if their vision resulted in a terrible product. At the very least, they saw something through.

A big thing that's different between how I do things now and how things were back then is where we started from. Our show started from me listening to old movie podcasts and wanting to do something similar. But we didn't come from a place of either actually having any kind of real expertise in game design or anything like that, and we weren't connected to any established networks or other podcasters or roleplaying game designer types.

Jon: Many of those movie podcasts were people in the industry.

Jef: And went to film school. You know, you look at *Flop House* or *We Hate Movies*, all of those guys are straight out of New York's film school system. So a lot of our terms that we were using from the early days were… I don't want to say wrong, but definitely made up by us. When we first met James D'Amato for the One Shot Network, he had us on *Critical Success*, that doesn't exist anymore. He wanted to interview us about the term "heartbreaker" under the assumption that we had enough connections to old Forge stuff to know what that is. And we, you know, everyone kind of knows the term heartbreaker,[1] but it turns out that we had a fundamentally different understanding of the term than either what is correct for it or what James wanted us to be talking about when we got on the show.

Jon: Yeah. It was a thing on The Forge, talking about games that was like, "It was heart breaking because it had one interesting idea in an otherwise terrible game.

Jef: And notably, I don't I'm not saying that by way of saying, "I always default to the Forge." The Forge is another thing that I didn't know what it was until I'd been making the show for 4 or 5 years. Just like John was talking about, with the breadth of experience leading to us kind of having a, like a fungal, rhizomatic, expertise of what games are like, because now we see all the threads and how every game is connected to every other game. We didn't know what that level of discourse was until we actually went back and researched Forge stuff, which was before our time. And we were like, "Wow, game reviews can get really stuffy."

B: And now that you're also doing *TV Mastery*, *Movie Mastery*, *Expounded Universe*, how has looking at different media, and reviewing all of that different stuff, affected, how you think of different like art forms and media?

Jef: For me at least, I feel like I'm so much more forgiving of a bad game than I am of a bad movie. But I don't know. I definitely do tend to think about one show while I'm making the others. But largely, it's just because there's stuff rattling around in my head. So if I recently watched a movie, I'm watching for parallels to that movie in a game I just reviewed, even though they shouldn't have anything to do with each other.

Jon: We one of the big things that's difficult with review, especially when it comes to specifically tabletop RPGs, is because there's such a long history, you know, especially for written media. But even for, you know, movies and television and things, there is a language of review and there is a language of quality that people understand. When you talk about the cinematography of a movie and people know what you're talking about, or if I talk about the language used in a book and how it used metaphor or something, people will know. "Okay, that's a thing that I understand and a way to talk about the quality of a book or a movie."

But in games, it's so much harder in a tabletop game specifically to talk about the quality of that, because so many people only view the quality of a game in terms of "how good is it when I play with my friend."

Jef: Yeah, that's a big thing that we deal with on a regular basis.

Jon: And it's the kind of thing where I go, you can hang out with your friends and have a good time no matter what, and it doesn't matter because I can hang out in a Denny's and have a great time. It doesn't mean Denny's is a Michelin star restaurant.

Jef: I guess we don't get that so much with movies. You never get the regular complaint that we get from RPGs that we're doing it wrong, that we do with movie reviews, because movie reviews don't have that level of kind of buffers of protection that people throw up, where when we're talking games, people often say, well, your game reviews don't count because you didn't play the game.

And we've always made it clear that we aren't even actively reviewing games. We're reviewing books. But ultimately, we think that we're pretty good at reviewing game play as an experience, too, because we do play a lot of games. We understand from reading them what the play experience would be like, what things guide and shape the play experience in the text.

But we see that complaint on a fairly regular basis that game reviews don't count unless you play the game. And then when you do play the game, game reviews don't count unless you play with a good DM. Yeah. And if you do play with a good DM, your DM is not as good as my DM. "My DM can make that game fun."

Jon: Or it's you played a bad [character] build. "That build was overpowered or underpowered" or whatever. There's always a qualifier in these where if someone likes a game a lot, there's not that level where someone will go, "It's a guilty pleasure of mine." They'll understand that some movie or TV or whatever property is known to not be particularly good, and they won't invest their own level of "this is a thing that it needs to be good for me to be good."

And so they'll go, "It's a guilty pleasure. This isn't great, but I like it anyway." I love watching *Supernatural*. It's a bad show, but I think it's great.

Jef: That said, I do think there's a place for that level of argument against critique in movies. It's just that we haven't reviewed those types of movies. Like if we were to do a "straight, no chaser" review of *Rocky Horror Picture Show*, people would rightly point out, "Well, you haven't seen it in a screaming, old theater hall full of half-naked people. The same thing if you reviewed a bootleg of a Phish concert. Well, that's got nothing on actually being at a Phish concert. So I can see where there are media critiques, but we just haven't touched those kinds of media.

B: Jef, you mentioned that you're more forgiving of a bad game than a bad movie. I think that's true of people in general. Why do you think that is?

Jef: It's funny, I started this conversation out by talking about how we kind of had to build our own expertise, and that's definitely been true of movie stuff as well because neither of us are film school people. But I do listen to more than my fair share of bad movie podcasts, and so just listening to those has taught me to identify dropped frames or people violating the 180° rule, which took me forever to even understand.

Now, because I spent so much time listening to those adopting their language and so on, it's made me the kind of person who watches movies that way. "Shoot, they changed horses between scenes, right?" Even though I don't want to be, I really wish I could go back.

Jon: I also think in games you have a level of control. If you see a thing where the movie did a thing wrong—"I don't like the way they made that shot or the way they delivered that line"—you can't change the movie. In a game, if you don't like a rule, you can change that rule.

Jef: That's true. Although, since I'm investing my time in these from the point of view of a reviewer, the reason I'm reading the game, is to discuss it later. Not to play it or fix it. A big part of it for me is, if I encounter a part of a book that I know full well what this is like, I can just say, "I don't need to read this." I see the start of a timeline that starts 40,000 years ago in a sci-fi dimension. I'm going to skip until it's not timeline formatted anymore. I'll just say it has a long timeline in it. And I can't do that with movies. If I skip ahead through the movie, I'm not reviewing it correctly. No one will ever catch me doing that on a book unless someone recorded me saying I did.

[Pensive silence]

B: I know y'all also play video games and other kinds of tabletop games. What do you want from them that's different from what you want from RPGs?

Jon: When I sit down to a board game as opposed to a RPG, I'm there for the puzzle of it more than anything, I like to figure out, "How does this mechanically work? What is the way that it needs to function? How do I do this in the best way?" I'm very much there to see the wheels, how it works, and try to do it as well as possible.

In an RPG, I do enjoy playing with the mechanics a lot, but I'm there to do like the roleplaying thing. I want to have fun in a world. It's for narrative purposes. It's such a different level of what I want out of something, like it scratches a different itch. The RPG is for my writer brain, and the board game is for the math brain.

Jef: And I think I've been thinking about this quite a bit, and a lot of the time it's the same for me. If I'm playing my old *Final Fantasy*, JRPG-type [Japanese RPG] stuff, then I'm just as much of an optimizer there as I am with my *D&D* character builds. But there are certain changes.

I tend to invest myself more heavily in my character if there's an audience to care, which means that as much as I like that you can make a Tav in *Baldur's Gate 3* ["Tav" is the default name for the player's character], I'm never going to start speaking in character. If I'm running a Tav character in the create-a-character build, I'm just not invested in that personality because who's there to be impressed? You won't see me saying lines to my computer screen and talking to Karlach. Tav's just a bundle of mechanics and the other three NPC's in the party, those are the ones that matter. I tend to get more invested in computer RPGs if the main character is not a build-your-own because I'm along for the story, especially if I can optimize them anyway.

Jon: I think at that point it does start to blur that line with the RPG versus a board game or anything like that, because then you really do start to go, "Well, this is about the narrative now more than just mechanics." So when you have something like *Baldur's Gate 3*, where you make your own character and that's sort of a little bundle of mechanics that hangs out with the narrative. Whereas if you look at something like, say, a *Mass Effect* or whatever, there's a big narrative thing that is getting pushed through here, and I'm making narrative choices for that. And I mean, even then your character is still just kind of a bundle of mechanics.

Jef: What's easier to get invested in? Shepard [the main character of *Mass Effect*] or Nameless Hero? Because everyone in the [game] world has an opinion about Shepard. So I yeah, I can see that. I'm not quite sure that that one would hold up to super intense scrutiny and argument. People would point out that, yeah, *Baldur's Gate 3* actually gives a lot of attention to your nameless main character. But I'm never going to speak in their voice, whereas if I'm sitting at my friend's table playing the *Sentinels of the Multiverse* roleplaying game and I've got a hero? Absolutely I'm going to come up with their voice. I know what their favorite songs are. I know all this stuff about them, but I would never bother with for my *Baldur's Gate 3* character, so I'm not sure where that difference comes from, but there certainly is one.

B: I was really surprised by how much mainstream success *Baldur's Gate 3* had. Just playing it, I was like, "Okay, if I didn't already know how to play *D&D*, this would be inscrutable." Did you have a similar experience? What was your reaction to *Baldur's Gate 3* happening?

[*Baldur's Gate 3* uses *Dungeons & Dragons* rules and world.]

Jon: I think people are willing to delve into a lot and forgive a lot when you give them some sexy blorbos to hang out with, and the… I mean, we have been on record as not being the biggest *D&D* boosters around, but one of the few things that [*D&D*] Fifth Edition at least has done is, at the very early levels, there's not a lot going on. So starting the game and going, "You have to start at level one. And then you're going to meet the same characters. And I feel like most people I know started and then quit and then restarted that game over and over and over again--

Jef: —Until they found a comfortable main character.

Jon: They're like, "Oh, I don't know if I want to play this class. Okay, I'll go through the intro, get off the ship, and then come back and start a new one." And so doing that, you're like, "Well, I figured out what I wanted to play, but I also just got comfortable with how Lae'zel is going to work, how Shadowheart is going to work. And so you kind of get the first levels of them figured out. Then you know how a couple spellcasting things work, how to do some martial maneuvers. You don't have a ton of things, but you do have a few, and it does like just kinda drip a few extra things every time, so it is good at giving you that.

And I think Larian did a great job of taking some of the *D&D* stuff and going, "Let's make this not as bad as it is in the tabletop version and make it work much better."

Jef: Yeah, I've been trying for a couple of minutes now to picture what it would be like to play it as someone who hadn't played *Baldur's Gate 1* and *2* and *D&D* for my whole life. And yeah, that would be a weird, vaguely inscrutable game. But I had also been thinking about my experience playing it, which was playing it as a person who genuinely doesn't like Fifth Edition very much. And one of the things I noticed right away is having a bit of an expertise in what *D&D* is and how people design games and a lot of knowledge about Fifth Edition, even if I don't like it very much, meant that the moment I booted the game up, I recognized kindred spirits. "Oh wow. People at Larian also don't like the Fifth Edition rule set. They fixed a lot of this."

B: You mentioned trends and patterns of thinking and design earlier. What are some of the stubborn ideas you'd like to see disappear? And what are some out of fashion ideas you would like to see return?

Jef: I am a big fan of games that are built around the idea that roles are going to be fluid. Like John mentioned earlier that in in *BG3*, when you play it, you have a natural tendency to start over a lot of times as you try and find your way into settle into a character you like. That has been my experience, not just with that game, but with tabletop roleplaying games. Once I establish, "oh, this character has three buttons they can push, and I pressed all three," I'm I'm very invested in immediately running off and trying another character out.

And that also applies to roles, things like tanks and controllers and people who are modifying the battlefield in certain ways. So I like it when you can swap those pieces out. And not just that, but also roles at the table. I like games that have fluid DM systems, and I think a lot of game designers are allergic to that. You see occasional halting pushes in the direction of a round robin style DM. I think that so far we've seen it largely as a kludge, and I'd like to see more games built around the core idea that who the DM is, is going to change from game to game, and it's going to be okay.

Largely because for me, a big part of what makes gaming culture kind of feel bad from time to time is that there's a lot of adherence to secrets at the table being a good idea. You see a lot of that in the OSR [Old School Renaissance or Revival] scene in older games. "My character is going to be evil, but I don't need the party to know. In fact, it's important they don't. So I have little secrets here and there." And that that kind of thing always bugs me because the roleplaying in roleplaying is like a play. And in plays, you know the dialog, and it doesn't mean that it you don't look surprised when you find out that your brother died in the play.

It's acting. It's an excuse for acting and challenges. So for me, I like it better when there aren't secrets, or if you want your character to have a secret from the other characters, that's great, but the players know so that they can play it up so they can lean into it. And games that support that structure of being open at the table, being honest at the table, and trusting your other players to play with that information.

Jon: Yeah, that is a big thing, the whole "GM as the authority figure and they have all the information and they'll let you know when it's time to know certain things."

Jef: Yeah. There's a lot of deference to the GM I would happily see done away with.

Jon: Yeah. And the GM running everything has been pulled back a bit more in recent years. You've gotten more games saying, no, this is a collaborative game and that includes the world building and how things are made. It isn't just you show up and you have a character and the GM did everything else. The idea that, no, this should be a collaborative effort with everyone, you can figure out what the world is like, what your town is like, what the NPC's are like.

Like Jef was saying, you can want to help create a villain and even know what they're doing and what their motivation is. You don't need to surprise me with, "Aaaaahhhhh! It turns out that this person is actually going to betray you!" It's fine. We can have that be a thing where we all act that out. But, if we collaboratively figure out what would be a cool way for the characters and story arc to go, both the player and GM will like it.

I'd like to see that happen. Then if I do have that and oh yeah, it turns out my mentor's actually evil and they're going to betray me, that's the thing I want to have happen. Then you and the GM are both on board. You get to have a cool moment, they get to do a cool villain thing, and everything's great. But if it's just a surprise from your GM, "That mentor that you've fully invested in is actually a villain, and now you don't get to see them anymore." You're like, "What the..? What are you talking about? I just put five points into this guy. What do you mean, he's a villain?"

Jef: The classic [RPG publisher] White Wolf, specifically Exalted-era White Wolf, problem where the more points you invest in something, the worse it is for you. Because it's super powerful and the game does not want you to start with something super powerful. So they come up with checks and balances. Except the checks outweigh the strength in the first place. When you do the mentor, a [rank] three mentor is perfect. He's a guy who hangs around and teaches you stuff. If you need to learn stuff, a rank one mentor is useless because he doesn't know anything; a five dot mentor is useless because he's inaccessible by design. But then why not just have the scale end at three. And start at three?

There are certain games that have done extremely cool stuff in the GM design space, although they aren't well-known games. I already mentioned *Sentinels of the Multiverse*, a personal favorite, does an amazing job of divorcing mechanics from narrative so your powers look like whatever you want. They just use a single mechanical sentence to activate and all the role playing is up to you. You rewrite the titles of them as much as you want. You choose what powers you're infusing into those abilities. It's a re-skinner's dream game, and I like that because I'm a natural born re-skinner. [Here, "skin" refers to elements of the game that don't affect how the rules function]

I feel like if you invent a mechanic that's "roll a d12" as the entire mechanic, I don't feel like another character class needs a much more convoluted version of something that, mathematically, is "roll a d12" just so the classes feel different.

Jon: Yeah, and *Spectaculars* has the role card you pick at the start of the session so if you want to be a tactician for this session, you aren't locked into being that. You can say, "Great. I was a tactician. Next session I can go ahead and be a support [character] and I'll still have my same powers. I'm still the same character, but the way in which I use my powers changes so that even though I still fundamentally look the same, I can still play different roles. I think that's a good way to keep things fresh and rolling in a different way.

Jef: That one's particularly good because you can choose at the start of each session. If you feel like being the guy who does AOE [area of effect] bombing attacks this session, you pick that role card of the 8 of them.

I thought that was genius. But there is a sort of not-quite-missing link between that and Fourth Edition *D&D*, which was the one to really codify those roles, which is *Strike! the RPG* by Jim McGarva. You choose one of like ten classes in the game for the combat model, but you also choose one of five roles. And so, instead of rogues always being strikers like they were back in Fourth Edition, now you say, "I'm a rogue, but I want to be a tank rogue, or I want to be an AoE damage rogue." So I like that because it broadens use case.

One of the more common complaints you saw about the fighter in Fourth Edition, back when the edition war was an ongoing concern, was how come they have to be defenders? Why? I used to make two-handed fighters all the time who just did damage. Here's your solution: the *Strike RPG*. Check that out. I like that, anything that gives me the tools to control how I'm going to narratively affect the game and how I'm going to mechanically affect the game, and I can choose both different versions of both. That's a favorite thing for me.

We had another half to that question, though.

B: Yes. What's something out of fashion is you would like to see return?

Jon: I mean, I know that this is sort of going against me criticizing the GM having all the knowledge and no one else, but I fucking love the idea of the GM being like, "I'm going to put on my fucking wizard robe and I'm going to stand behind a filing cabinet and talk about shit." I love the idea of the theatrics that early roleplaying games had. "I'm going to like really bring the lights down low and I'm going to have my full like GM voice and I'm going to get behind this thing so you can't see me and I'm going to narrate stuff." The level of taking this too seriously that very early roleplaying had before people started to make fun of it.

And then they were like, "Oh no, we have to be serious, because now everyone thinks we're nerds and we don't want people to look down on us." But that was fucking great. That ruled. I loved that theater kid energy.

Jef: Yeah, I can't think of much mechanically that I really wish would come back because honestly, the evolution of RPGs from the 70s to now has been largely, fairly positive. No doubt a lot of stuff was bad, a lot of it I don't want to see return.

One thing I do kind of miss in terms of readability of RPGs is I liked how much they used to be much more like the singular visions of crazy people in their garages. To the point where you'd be reading a roleplaying game about, like, fantasy Europe or something and then halfway through there would be three paragraphs on the realities of four wheel drive engines and dune buggies. And the guy would be like, "This is all according to my friend Dune Buggy Dan. Here's his address if you have any questions." Oh man, the 70s, when you just publish your friend Dune Buggy Dan's address.

Jon: I feel like that's almost made a comeback now with zine culture. Before you'd be reading an RPG and at the end of it they'd go, "And if you have questions, send a letter to my home address. Ask me if you want anything and maybe I'll include your question in the next edition of my game."

That's insane! You'd see that and it's, you know, the late 1990s, early 2000s, the most ridiculous thing you've ever seen. Now, it's at this point where I'll buy some RPG off the Internet and the author will say, "Great, and here's my handle and just ask me anything and I don't care." The level of transparency got so opaque for a while, and then it went right back.

Jef: I like that little bit of idiosyncrasy you'd see in older games. Like if you were to ask me if I'd rather play, say, *Fifth Cycle*, which is an old 80s RPG, a *D&D* rip off, or *Mörk Borg*, which is a critical darling nowadays, obviously, I'd rather play *Mörk Borg*. It's a well-designed game that looks like a [Trader Joe's] Fearless Flier. It's pretty, but, would I rather read *Mörk Borg* or *Fifth Cycle*? I'd rather read *Fifth Cycle*. It's nuts. It's a delight.

Or *Bunnies and Burrows*. Yeah. I would rather read *Bunnies and Burrows* than just about anything. It's only 30 pages long, and those 30 pages are crammed with the craziest stuff you've ever seen. Would I play it? No, it's virtually unplayable. It was written by veterinarians who had only heard of *D&D*, but, you know, it's fun to read.

B: That brings to mind something that I've been encountering on my research for the book: how people think about authorship. And a lot of that is how we define art. I guess my question is, how do games relate to art or artistry, and what how do you define those, and what is your role in those definitions as critics?

Jef: So I guess the question is, we start with a baseline, "Is a roleplaying game an artistic work?" And I would say 100%, yeah, it absolutely is. It's a work of creative writing and it takes a tremendous amount of work to write one. You need to know, or at least you're ostensibly supposed to know, how your pieces interact, what the end goal is and, and what it should look like if people sit down to play a session. I think that when you're critiquing, one of the first things you point out is: they didn't. They didn't.

They wrote this without stopping. They didn't think how any part of this game interacts with any other part of this game. That doesn't mean it's less of an artwork, like one of my favorite old games that we've read that no one else has ever heard of is called *The Great War of Magellan* by Richard Hatch, who won a season of survivor and was on *Battlestar Galactica*. Like the original, the 70s one. Interesting guy. The game is a standard space piracy, rebels versus empire-type situation. The rules are terrible. Absolutely terrible. But it is a delight to read because it's obviously this guy's vision. Not only was it his vision to make an RPG, but it was going to be his media empire. He was going to make a show called *The Great War of Magellan*.

B: I remember your review of that. There's sort of…pitch deck materials in the rulebook or something like that, right?

Jef: Yeah, yeah, yeah. And I actually saw it before it got scoured for the internet entirely. I managed to locate the trailer that he had filmed with his own money. Which had almost nothing to do with the game. Like, they were unrecognizable to each other. I could only find it on an unmaintained Facebook page. It's been cleaned up, and I would do anything to get it back again.

But yeah, we definitely think of roleplaying games as artistic endeavors. I think that's a big part of how we critique them. Are they fun to read? Do they have a flow? Do they have a point? I guess it's kind of a bad thing to ask if art has a point. I should say rather, "Do they have a vision?" Do they have a vision of what the game flow is going to be, or what the reading flow is going to be like? That's a big part of how I critique them.

A lot of the time when we review games, we say, "Why was this written? What were they mad about when they wrote this?" I know that's a reductive way of saying it, but a lot of the old indie games people were mad about *D&D* when they wrote those games.

Jon: I think a lot of games, especially modern games, have taken the idea of "a game as art" as a thing that they very much like to resonate with. We brought up Mörk Borg as a thing that is not just in the gameplay, but in the presentation, how the game is delivered, is an art piece itself. But I think even devoid of art entirely, if you just have like a straight up word document of a game, stripped of everything else. You still have the artistic expression there because you have the idea of not just play in the way that you would if I gave you the technical rules to basketball. Technically it tells you how to play a game, the rules for it. But I would never call the manual for how to play basketball "art," but so much of RPGs is a personal experience that gets translated into not only mechanics, but the world they are placed into, the assumptions that are placed into game play.

We bring up a lot about how the mechanics inform gameplay, or when I am asked to make certain roles, or when the game assumes you will be doing certain things. How does this inform how I am supposed to play? You know, like the main, big, typical example being *Dread* with the Jenga tower and the sort of nervousness and anxiety that comes from pulling a tile from a tower that's already been prepped, even from the start, to be slightly wobbly.

The *Dread* book doesn't really have any art in it, but it is an art piece. It is so evocative of emotion, even just reading it before you play, you understand how this is supposed to happen. Being able to convey that in the written form, I think, is an artistic function of an RPG.

B: Part of why I'm interested in these tensions is, so often when people talk about video games and they critique video games, they sort of talk about them like a product review, or sort of a designed object for a goal.

In y'all's work, you can look at something like *F.A.T.A.L.* [seriously, don't look up this one] and call the game fascist and out-of-its-mind hateful. But there's this moratorium in video games of actually addressing what a thing is about. I guess I'm curious if you have any thoughts on why that might be.

Jon: I mean, it's a little harder, I suppose, with an RPG to get into that. Like a lot of people love to project that into fiction, where you can do narrative analysis say it's about something else. "Oh, this story is actually about capitalism;" "This story is actually about whatever." You can make an argument, you look at specific things, say this is a stand in for that. And when you look at an RPG which doesn't have as much of a straight narrative to it, it's much harder to say something stands in for something.

A lot of times we've reviewed things and very obviously someone is doing this because of whatever. Like *Broncosaurus Rex*: this person had opinions about the Civil War.

Jef: Oof I was thinking of *DragonRaid*. It's pretty famous at this point as a game that was written as *D&D* from first principles by people who would not read *D&D* for religious reasons but wanted to make their own, and it very much has its heart on its sleeve. It has rules in it that are straight up the tactics used in conversion therapy as game mechanics. Which is a wild swing to exist at all, let alone to still exist: you can still go by that, new.

I think, yeah, certain games are easier to critique when they have their heart on their sleeve, and it's less interesting to me to even talk about them when they're like, oh, like when you talk about *Phoenix Command*. The company, Leading Edge, all their games are extremely simulation-like. The whole gimmick of the game is when you shoot a bullet, you're going to measure things like gravity and wind speed and deviation and imperfections of rifling in the barrel. But there are people who are into that, you know, just like there are people who want to play that board game *Campaign for North Africa* where a turn takes three weeks.

Those games are almost completely unreviewable for me because I'm just not the right kind of person to even understand what I'm reading, let alone have an opinion on it.

Jon: I think when it comes down to it, people are much more willing to argue their position on media and what its narrative means than with RPGs.

I also think the whole transparency thing has also been detrimental to that a bit, because if I have an opinion about whatever game and what it's about, that designer is probably on social media and someone can just immediately tag them and ask, "Hey, is this game about this?" And they can say yes or no and give their opinion. And the thing is, you could do the exact same thing with a movie. I could say, "I think this movie is actually about how war is bad," and the director can say, "I was never thinking about that at all when I made this movie. That has nothing to do with it."

You constantly see people going, "Oh, that's [the author's] opinion. [Roland Barthes'] 'Death of the Author'." In RPGs, we haven't gotten to the point where people are willing to take a stand on something like that. I don't know if it's because it's a newer medium that people are more deferential or if it's because of the nerd fallacy: I don't want to be upsetting to anyone else, ever. I want to be as nice as possible.

Jef: I think one of the key things you can evaluate when you're discussing this, obviously, is [*D&D* co-creator] Gary Gygax, who was an important person in early RPG development and also lived long enough to become one of those weirdo message board posters.

He died in 2008. In like 2007, he was still just openly saying the dumbest things you could possibly think of in message boards. Just happily saying, "I was thinking about Commodore Shillington from the American Civil War when I wrote about Lawful Good Paladins. You know, the guy who did all those Native massacres?" He was still online saying that stuff.

So nowadays we don't have to do a "Death of the Author" because you can look right at all the things he said in his life, all his letters, all his weird opinions about women in gaming and how their brains aren't right. And all the stuff he was saying right up until he died. But you can also go on different message boards and watch people, in real time, try to apologize for that stuff to go, "He didn't mean that. He was… he was actually talking about something different. You know, ultimately he was a troubled or confusing person, but the important thing is, he did write *D&D.* Well, probably. We're not sure. Might have been Arneson."

Granted, we have kind of entered an era where now, if you texted Ryan Johnson about a "Benoit Blanc" movie, it's not all that unlikely that he'll respond to you. He'll happily say, "I'm not going to make one with the Muppets. I can't think of how to do it." We've entered a homogenization age. I don't think you'd be able to get Francis Ford Coppola to tell you anything about *Megalopolis,* but you can get Jordan Peele to talk.

B: What's a game that needs a new edition or needs a remake? A game that has an idea that's so good, but the execution just wasn't there?

Jon: You know, it's hard because so often when I think of old games that might have had a good idea, most of the time I think, a lot of modern games can do that. Any genre you can think of has had a decent game in it, so it almost always ends up coming down to specific properties that you would want. Because if there was a really cool Western game and they had some neat ideas and then they fumbled it, well, yeah, but there are several cool Western games I could play.

Jef: Name one.

B: Dogs in—

Jef: Hard mode: no *Dogs in the Vineyard.*

B: Damnit.

Jon: I honestly was thinking, I would have loved to have seen an actual, not *D&D*-based *World of Warcraft* RPG. All we got was a [*D&D*] Third Edition shovelware. And *WoW* has so much stuff in it at this point. And being a Fourth Edition, the MMO for babies apologist as I am, the concept of taking the good things about MMO's and making an RPG out of it and really stick to the ideas of the MMO...It has 20 years of content to go through. You can do all the different expansions. You've got so much stuff, you've got so many classes, it has so many things you could do with it. That would be so easy. If Blizzard ever wanted to make a Kickstarter, it would make several million dollars immediately. And there are several designers that would just jump at the chance to do that, and they would be so cheap. Yeah.

Jef: I'm going to go with a pretty easy answer here. The game already has six editions of the main game and two editions of the quickplay version, one that just recently got kickstarted. All of them, all six of them, have the best story ever. But are the worst game ever. And that's *Shadowrun*. I have six editions of *Shadowrun* sitting here and I won't play a single one of them for any amount of money because they're two fiddly and they get in your way instead of getting out of your way when you want to run cyberpunk stuff.

I think Shadowrun has a unique vision in terms of cyberpunk gaming because it adds in all that weird fantasy stuff and Dragon CEO's and all this other stuff that's not just doing a *Neuromancer*- or *Altered Carbon*-type storyline. Everyone knows Shadowrun. They know right off the top of the heads, "I'm gonna make an orc decker, I'm going to make a cool dwarf."

And then they actually start trying to play the game. And it is the most obtuse pile of sacred cow rules. And whenever they put out a new edition, they add parts to it that don't fit with the other parts, and all the balance is thrown off. And there are whole books of guns! There doesn't need to be any of that.

They put out *Anarchy*, which is supposed to be a GM-less or round robin GM-controlled fast play game. Character assembly is theoretically faster because they removed the priority system, but at the same time, they also tried to get you to not even bother with character creation by having a full third of the book be pre-gen characters. It's insane. The gameplay isn't even faster. It's the same gameplay. You're still picking up giant 20 plus handfuls of d6's, rolling them, and then going through and fiddly picking out each one of the relevant rolls and comparing them against a million modifiers.

I love the story of Shadowrun, the concept, the vibe that it implies by suggesting so much stuff is happening in the Pacific Northwest, and dragons being everywhere, and mercenaries, and the whole wetwork angle of trying to steal corporate talent away for other corporations. The 80s-ness of it all. The fact that it's still very much like all cyberpunk: convinced that the Japanese are going to suddenly reclaim their technological glory from the 80s. Yet the games have been consistently unplayable.

Just give me one that doesn't have all these sacred cows. One "modern sensibilities" version. Sure, it gets new editions all the time, it's the publisher's cash cow. But I just want one version that I like. Virtually any other game that's got a million editions, I like one of them.

B: That's it from me. Is there anything you want to share, to impart to game designers of the of the next generation?

Jef: Do a dinosaur game. Yeah.

Jon: Do a backflip. No, honestly, I'm just so excited about the way the hobby is currently going. Over the last ten years or so, things have gotten so good. Roleplayers have it so good right now. The amount of games, the breadth of games, the depth of games that have been coming out over the past ten years have been astounding, especially as people who have been reviewing as much as we have. In the 90s, in the 80s, there were a ton of RPGs, way more than people think, that were published, but so many of them were just the same sort of thing. No one was taking risks, and if they did, the risks weren't very much worth it.

Jef: Like the OGL [Open Gaming License] era?

Jon: You had that and then you had someone: "Oh, I've got my own idea!" No, it was the same idea.

Jef: "What if it's *D&D* but the combat's harder?"

Jon: "*D&D*, but I added a weird rule for armor for some reason, or a new faith system because all of the religions they put in were fake!" And nowadays, I can want a game that's very specifically about a thing, or a game that I know is only going to be for a specific audience, or is only ever going to be played like twice ever because it's so heavy. Having these kind of almost bespoke experiences is great because it starts letting the hobby become like the other media. Once you have a huge explosion of choices and types and genres and versions of these games out there, then you can start to have a language develop better, like you have for video games, TV and movies, and you can have people engage with it in a way that isn't just "I play *D&D*, and *D&D* is the only thing I know, and that's the only thing there is." When you have games as huge and varied and good and interesting as we've been getting recently, I think it can only be good for the hobby.

Jef: And I think that, you know, part of it is also that smaller games are seeing a moment in a way that they never have in the past, and I appreciate that. I was just reading this morning about a new game, *Under Hill, By Water.* And it is literally, "What if you just played the first chapter of *Fellowship of the Ring*?" It's just "Concerning Hobbits, the Roleplaying Game." You never go on a quest. The only point of the game is to see who can grow a big carrot and get drunk and fall asleep in a garden.

And I'm like, "What a great idea!" It's just playing as cozy Hobbits in a cozy Hobbit village without having to write the entirety of an army like *MERP* [*Middle Earth Role Playing*] because you don't need to worry about a Balrog's stats. You just need to worry about what the Sackville Baggins are getting up to. I love that and also for me, the small games, I've really been enjoying those.

Also, I like the retro clone spirit I've been seeing in the past couple of years. We're all used to people rewriting *D&D*, but *Mutants in the Now* is a retro clone of *Teenage Mutant Ninja Turtles and Other Strangeness* and *After the Bomb.* A Palladium game! Who, up until just a few years ago, who would have even thought to bother? Why would you bother making a retro clone of a game that captured 4% of the market share at its highest point? It's because people love those games and there is a lot of memory of them, even if everybody read them and then played *D&D*, the knowledge of those games exists, and the fact that there's enough out there nowadays, enough players and enough brand identity, to support things like that is great.

So if there's a weird old game that you would like to do a rewrite of, do it. The market's there. I like the retro clone movement and I like games that really focus in on a vibe, on a specific little moment. *Under Hill, By Water* reminded me of *Golden Sky Stories* because right away it's just like, "What do you do in this game? I play as a cute little critter, and I wander around a quaint Japanese village, and I help kids. And if a real problem arises, that's bad because that's not what my job is."

Jon: Or *The Time We Have*, a two-player RPG where you're brothers and one of you is infected with the zombie virus, and it is your final goodbye and holy shit, that is the fucking…like goddamn. And the infected person, as you're setting up the game physically, they write a goodbye letter to the other player and you may or may not actually hand that over. You might not actually even do that. Just like, this fucking rules! And the art! It is gorgeous.

It's the kind of thing where you could own this and never play it, and it would still be worth purchasing. Reading through it, looking at the art, it's amazing as a thing to own, even if you never play it. That's exactly what I want to see: stuff made that is just beautiful ideas.

Jef: I think a big part of what makes games like that work at all, like, *Ten Candles* or the one you were just mentioning, is the explosion of the convention scene. It's much harder to imagine playing *The Time We Have* with your friends over and over and over again, but playing with strangers once? A delight.

But anything can be a game. And anything should be a game. The fact that we reviewed *Dallas* and were amazed that it was genuinely good? Take that as a lesson. A war game company in 1980 which, prior to that, had only made games about the efficacy of certain types of tanks made a reasonably good LARP about the *Dallas* TV show. You could do anything. You can do it.

NOTE

1. "Heartbreaker" can refer either to a game similar to an RPG by that name or a game which is too much like *D&D* to find an audience. "The Forge" was an online RPG forum that has since shut down.

BIBLIOGRAPHY

Baculi, Spencer. "Sony Censors LGBT Content from Saudi Arabian Release of 'Marvel's Spider-Man 2.'" Bounding Into Comics, 17 Feb. 2024, boundingintocomics.com/video-games/sony-censors-lgbt-content-from-saudi-arabian-release-of-marvels-spider-man-2.

Badowsky, Adam, Tomaszkiewicz, Konrad, and Amatangelo, Gabriel. *Cyberpunk 2077.* CD Projekt Red, 2020.

Baker, Troy. "@TroyBakerVA." X (Formerly Twitter), 28 June 2020, x.com/TroyBakerVA/status/1277353529791770624?s=20.

"Banksy Brings down the House at the Contemporary Art Evening Auction." Sothebys.Com, 2 Mar. 2022, www.sothebys.com/en/articles/banksy-brings-down-the-house-at-the-contemporary-art-evening-auction?locale=en.

"Banksy Video Shows Plan to Shred Entire Girl with Balloon Artwork." *The Guardian*, Guardian News and Media, 18 Oct. 2018, www.theguardian.com/artanddesign/2018/oct/18/banksy-video-girl-with-balloon-shred-entire-artwork.

Bartz-Todd, Cathie A. "Cool Spot." Virgin Interactive Entertainment, 1993.

Benjamin, Walter. "The Work of Art in the Age of Mechanical Reproduction." *Illuminations*, Hannah Arendt, Frankfurt, 1969, pp. 1–26.

Bonk, Lawrence. "Shadow of Mordor's Innovative Nemesis System Is Locked behind a Patent until 2036." Engadget, Engadget, 26 Feb. 2025, www.engadget.com/gaming/shadow-of-mordors-innovative-nemesis-system-is-locked-behind-a-patent-until-2036-195437208.html.

Boone, Jim. *Saints Row 4*. Deep Silver, PlayStation 3, 2013.

Camus, Albert. *The Myth of Sisyphus and Other Essays*. Vintage International, New York, United States, 1991.

Chick, Jack T. *Dark Dungeons*. Chick Publications, California, United States, 1984.

Crawford, Jeremy, et al. Player's Handbook: Dungeons & Dragons: Everything a Player Needs to Create Heroic Characters for the World's Greatest Roleplaying Game. Wizards of the Coast LLC, 2014.

C-Span. User Clip: Pat Buchanan Ad Featuring Tongues Untied, C-SPAN, 11 Aug. 2017, www.c-span.org/clip/public-affairs-event/user-clip-pat-buchanan-ad-featuring-tongues-untied/4679699.

DeClara, Joe. "Cyberpunk 2077: 10 Most Hilarious Glitches People Have Reported." TheGamer, TheGamer, 28 Dec. 2020, www.thegamer.com/cyberpunk-2077-funny-glitches/.

Durantaye, Leland de la. "Readymade Remade: Leland De La Durantaye." CABINET, 2007, www.cabinetmagazine.org/issues/27/durantaye.php.

Doucet, Nicolas. "Astro Bot." Sony Computer Entertainment, 2024.

Ebert, Roger. "Okay, Kids, Play on My Lawn: Roger Ebert." RogerEbert.Com, 15 Dec. 2012, www.rogerebert.com/roger-ebert/okay-kids-play-on-my-lawn.

Eco, Umberto. "Ur-Fascism." The Anarchist Library, The New York Review of Books, 22 July 1995, theanarchistlibrary.org/library/umberto-eco-ur-fascism.

Eno, Brian. *A Year with Swollen Appendices*. Faber and Faber, London, United Kingdom, 1996.

"Episode 1." System Mastery. Systemmastery.com, 2013

Foddy, Bennett. "Getting over It with Bennett Foddy." 2017.

"Fortnite." Epic Games, 2017.

"FOX NEWS Mass Effect Sex Debate." YouTube, Fox News, www.youtube.com/watch?v=PKzF173GqTU. Accessed 15 Dec. 2025.

Greig, James. "Inside the Far Right's Growing Obsession with Art." Dazed, 21 July 2022, www.dazeddigital.com/art-photography/article/56588/1/inside-the-far-rights-growing-obsession-with-art-criticism-twitter-degenerate.

Hessel, Katy. "Katy Hessel: The Story of Art without Men." YouTube, Hirshhorn, 23 June 2023, www.youtube.com/watch?v=3byyI4G_5Ew.

"'In Rehearsals It Worked Every Time': Banksy on Incomplete Shredding of Girl With Balloon." YouTube, Guardian News, 2018, www.youtube.com/watch?v=TTqgVPHJeNY.

Kaga, Shouzou. "Fire Emblem: Genealogy of the Holy War." Nintendo, 1996.

Keeler, Ken. "A Star Is Burns." The Simpsons, season 6, episode 18, Fox, 5 Mar. 1995.

Kim, Matt. "Epic Games Boss Says All Politics Should Be Removed from Game Companies [Update]." IGN, 12 Feb. 2020, www.ign.com/articles/epic-games-boss-says-all-politics-should-be-removed-from-games.

Kusakihara, Toshiyuki & Yokota, Genki. "Fire Emblem: Three Houses." Nintendo, 2019.

Lazarus, Tom, director. *Mazes and Monsters*. McDermott Productions, United States, 1982.

LeGuin, Ursula K. "28. It Doesn't Have to Be the Way It Is." UrsulaK.LeGuin.Com, 12 Apr. 2023, www.ursulakleguin.com/blog/28-it-doesnt-have-to-be-the-way-it-is.

Litchfield, Ted. "A Veteran Final Fantasy Programmer Hates How Indie Games Deliberately Recreate PS1 Visual Bugs He Made 'many Futile Efforts' to Fix: 'I Just Don't Get What's so Interesting about Trying to Replicate That.'" PC Gamer, 11 Aug. 2025.

Maeda, Kouhei, & Yokoto, Genki. "Fire Emblem: Awakening." Nintendo, 2013.

Menkman, Rosa. "Glitch Studies Manifesto." Amsterdam, 2009.

Meta advertisement. *Ray-Ban/Meta Channel, YouTube*, February 3, 2025.

"Mom and Pop Art." *The Simpsons*, written by Al Jean and Tim Long, directed by Steven Dean Moor and Jim Reardon, Fox, 1999.

Michaels, Marguerite. "Anne Tyler, Writer 8:05 to 3:30." *The New York Times*, 8 May 1977.

"Never Alone: Video Games and Other Interactive Design | Moma." Museum of Modern Art, 2023, www.moma.org/calendar/exhibitions/5453.

Nochlin, Linda (1971). "Why Are There No Great Women Artists?". In Gornick, Vivian, and Moran, Barbara (eds.). *Woman in Sexist Society: Studies in Power and Powerlessness*. New York: Basic Books.

Ocule. "[List] TTRPG Guide to Woke Companies." TheRPGSite, 3 Aug. 2021, www.therpgsite.com/pen-paper-roleplaying-games-rpgs-discussion/list-ttrpg-guide-to-woke-companies/.

O'Hara, Jack. "*Call of Duty Modern Warfare. PlayStation 4*." Activision Publishing, Inc, 2019.

Persson, Johan. "*Battlefield 1*." Electronic Arts, Inc, 2016.

Plante, Chris. "The 50 Best Games of 2017." Polygon, Polygon.com, 18 Dec. 2017, www.polygon.com/2017-best-games/2017/12/18/16781674/best-video-games-2017-top-50-mario-pubg-zelda/.

"Pride Flags:: Marvel's Spider-Man 2 General Discussions." Steam Community, steamcommunity.com/app/2651280/discussions/0/599643178892580669/. Accessed 10 Dec. 2025.

Ratcatcher (1999). *The Criterion Collection*, www.criterion.com/films/716-ratcatcher. Accessed 13 Dec. 2025.

Ricciardi, Tiney. "'South Park' Creators on Newest Season: 'Politics Became Pop Culture.'" The Denver Post, 11 Nov. 2025.

Riggs, Marlon. "Tongues Untied." *The Signifyin' Works of Marlon Riggs*. Janus Films, United States, 2021.

Sontag, Susan. *Against Interpretation: And Other Essays*. Picador, New York, United States, 2025.

Sontag, Susan. *Under the Sign of Saturn*. Farrar, Straus, and Giroux, New York, United States, 1980.

"The Charnel House." PabloPicasso.org, https://www.pablopicasso.org/the-charnel-house.jsp.

Vesce, Sean, & Hope, Ishmael Angaluuk. "Never Alone." E-Line Media, 2014.

Warzel, Charlie. "How an Online Mob Created a Playbook for a Culture War." *The New York Times*, 15 Aug. 2019, www.nytimes.com/interactive/2019/08/15/opinion/what-is-gamergate.html.

Watson, Paul. "Why Modern Art Is Absolute Crap." YouTube, YouTube, 30 Mar. 2017, www.youtube.com/watch?v=PRWJcrRO0GM.

Whitaker, Forrest and Jarmusch, Jim. "Ghost Dog: The Way of the Samurai." Cinema Club, 2002.

"Who We Are." *Museum of the Moving Image*. Movingimage.org/about/.

Wilde, Oscar. *The Complete Works of Oscar Wilde*. HarperCollins Publishers, 2018.

Wilson, William. "Art Review: Revisiting the Unthinkable: Nazi Germany's 'degenerate Art' Show at LACMA." Los Angeles Times, Los Angeles Times, 15 Feb. 1991, www.latimes.com/archives/la-xpm-1991-02-15-ca-1169-story.html.

"Woman Who Bought Shredded Banksy Artwork Will Go through with Purchase." *The Guardian*, Guardian News and Media, 11 Oct. 2018, www.theguardian.com/artanddesign/2018/oct/11/woman-who-bought-shredded-banksy-artwork-will-go-through-with-sale.

Wood, Austin. "QWOP Successor Getting over It Is Now Available on Steam." PC Gamer, 6 Dec. 2017, www.pcgamer.com/qwop-successor-getting-over-it-is-now-available-on-steam/.

CHAPTER 2

But You Have Infinite Chances to Make a Post-Impression

Impressionist Play

My friend and colleague Prof. Fox Zarow liked to play *Zelda* as a kid. I don't just mean they liked to play *Zelda* video games, though that's true. What I mean is, they would wear a green tunic, grab a stick, and run around the woods, fighting imaginary bokoblin and like-likes (Mello-Klein). My brother and I did something similar, running around fields and pastures as the Mario Bros or Dash Rendar from *Star Wars: Shadows of the Empire*. As I got older and reflected on my video game proclivities, I realized it wasn't just that I wanted fun games with good stories. I wanted games with worlds I wanted to visit, even if I didn't want to live there. The first video game I remember getting on its own, as *Super Mario World* came packaged with the Super Nintendo, was the SNES version of *Batman Returns*. I was thrilled. I loved the movie and wanted to be in it. Only as Batman, though.

Hyrule, at least Young Link's Hyrule in *Ocarina of Time*, would be a splendid place to live. I know lots of people haven't played a *Zelda* game, since they're almost entirely for Nintendo systems, so a brief rundown: *The Legend of Zelda* almost always has players take on the role of Link as he rescues

DOI: 10.1201/9781003755821-2

Princess Zelda from the evil wizard Gannon. Pretty straightforward fairy tale fare. Link explores various temples, castles, etc. ("dungeon" is the catch-all term) to accumulate equipment for defeating bosses and solving puzzles. It's a lot of fun to play, but that's not necessarily where the game's charm lies.

Prof. Zarow said of the *Zelda* series in general that, "Even if you have one Zelda game as a kid and you didn't even beat it, there's still something about that story that you can relate to and makes people love it" (Mello-Klein). That remains the case with me and *Ocarina*, although I've seen the ending thanks to shared save files. The year it came out, 1998, I was the same age as Young Link as he sets out on his adventure. After three dungeons, there's a time skip to "Adult Link," laughably age 17. That's when I would lose steam. Once the game opened up, I got overwhelmed. It's not just *Zelda* that has so much more to do than games where Batman walks to the right and punches all clowns. *Ocarina of Time*'s map was huge. I had never seen anything like it before and, in case you haven't played games that old, the wayfinding was as annoying as it was unhelpful. Navi the fairy (yes, as in "navigate") would pester "Link!" to "Listen"! When the player did, Navi would say to go to such and such a place. Players with follow-up questions such as "where is that" or "yes, but how do I actually get in there," were fresh out of luck.

In a way, I didn't mind not finding my way around because I didn't really want to arrive. Adult Link's Hyrule was much more open and complex, so it had more to explore, but it was also a hellscape. Screeching zombies, a red and smoggy sky (not so different from some Gotham Cities), and a distinct lack of cute dogs in the town square. I wanted to live in Young Link's magical Kokiri Forest and visit Lon Lon Ranch. I wanted to explore and solve simple dungeons and fight merely inconvenient enemies. Most of my *Ocarina of Time* playing was, and I'm not alone in this, spent somersaulting around Hyrule Field. For me, *Ocarina of Time* is, more than anything else, the feeling I had when I first met Zelda standing on a dais in her garden. It's the same shot used for the game's "The End" screen, and that's perfect: *Ocarina of Time's* elegiac epilogue expanded how I felt about games.

The perfect counterpoint to that feeling was *OoT*'s contemporary, and one of my favorite games of all time, *Final Fantasy VII*. The *Final Fantasy* series is something of an anthology, and only a few games have a direct sequel, though *VII* has a bevy of sequels, prequels, side-stories, and even a movie. Historically, *Final Fantasy* games took design cues from games like *Dungeons & Dragons*: stats that determine other stats, lots of equipment to fiddle around with, and turn-based battles. These games had either a swords and sorcery setting or one with magic and esoteric technology.

Final Fantasy VII embraced science fiction with its urban setting and cyberpunk themes of corporate oppression. *FFVII* opens in dystopic Midgar City (another *Final Fantasy* hallmark is its grab bag of names from different mythologies). You could say Midgar is two cities. One is elevated and home to the comfortable classes, especially those who work for the real power in Midgar, the Shinra Electric Power Company. Beneath the upper crust, which one character describes as "that &^$ 'pizza," are the slums. Down there, it's basically *Blade Runner*'s LA but less rainy because the sky is blocked. Anyway, the game starts with players committing an act of ecoterrorism. When the camera pulls out and the reactor explosion seems small compared to the rest of the city, the sense of scale can't help but impress. In terms of play time, Midgar is maybe 15% of the game, but its claustrophobic, oppressive, and often sleazy streets loom large in players' minds.

As *FFVII*'s world opens up, players visit the characters' hometowns and learn their backstories. It's a wild cast. There's a talking dog, a vampire, and a remote-controlled cat doll and *it* pilots a giant plushie. There are humans, too. One of them has a machine gun for an arm. *FFVII* was so weird and evocative that I fell in love with it instantly. It was my first game with a story of real consequence and the first game that made me cry.

OoT and *FFVII* both revel in showing off their forests, fields, and mountains. They delight in the occult with their shadowy castles or mansions. They are stories of unclear parentage, and their characters blur gender roles. These two titles, and a lot of role-playing games, share a lot of themes with Romantic art. This isn't "romance" in the sense of love stories. Romanticism is interested in love, but as part of the natural world and its drama. This is the kind of romance meant in *Romance of the Three Kingdoms* and the various Koei Tecmo video game series inspired by it (e.g., *Dynasty Warriors*).

"Romance" is, like any genre, art movement, or school of thought, kind of a loose term. While it includes Mary Shelley's *Frankenstein* and Guillermo del Toro's film adaptation of her novel, I would not include the old Universal movies directed by James Whale. Those are wonderful, it's just that they're horror films. Romanticism in literary and visual arts did often address the horrifying, driving to the point that Nature is unfeeling and unthinking. Sometimes, so too are humans.

Even so, I don't think *Ocarina of Time* and *Final Fantasy VII* are romances, exactly. I'm sticking to my guns on using how it feels to play a game, rather than its audio/visual components, to "read" it, but formal elements are part of the feel. In visual arts, Romanticism was largely concerned with capturing landscapes, and how the artist interpreted "appearances in relation to certain human values" (Bourde 8). You could ask how a Romantic might use the image of a forest or cliff side to address "beauty" or "eternity." These things don't exist in the world; humans use the world to create them. It's a human mind that sees a rainbow (or what-have-you) and ascribes beauty to it. *OoT* and *FFVII* are different in that they are not interested in you forgetting that they're video games.

Impressionism (and Post-Impressionism) focused less on finding the beauty in nature and more on conveying the impressions the world afforded the artist *en plein air* (because of course we need to make "outside" sound fancy). Daubs of paint and brush strokes are clearly visible; they'd have to be to "spontaneously" capture a lovely tableau. The materials were not made to mimic reality. Viewers, like the painter, got the impression of things through form and color.

The polygonal graphics from the PlayStation/Nintendo 64 era, with the fidelity to suggest things like humans and trees, weren't a creative choice. I'm not using the visibility of the medium, like daubs of paint on a canvas, to align these older games with Impressionism. And at the time, *Ocarina of Time* and *Final Fantasy VII* looked more realistic to us than games ever had before. Now it's apparent to me that I was filling in a lot of details with the help of instruction booklet illustrations, but even with 3-D space and polygonal models, *OoT* and *FFVII* were stylized. *Ocarina*, built in the same engine as *Super Mario 64* ("Interview"), had a kind of bulbous, storybook look approximating sprites used in previous *Zelda* games and their anime/manga feel.

FFVII was also the first in its series to use 3D models, although it didn't actually have 3D environments. The developers used prerendered gifs to save memory and processing power. *VII* blended "chibi" style characters in gameplay with videos using more realistic models. Up to this point, *Final Fantasy* had been on Nintendo consoles, but Squaresoft jumped ship because they wanted to make those fully rendered cutscenes. The chibi or "super-deformed" style is common in Japanese comics and anime, and I had seen similar art styles in cell animation and video game sprites, but I didn't know what to make of it when I saw it in 3D. At first, I thought I was supposed to understand that the characters looked like children, so I was confused when they looked more realistic in combat and cinematic cutscenes. This blend of styles, combined with Yoshitaka Amano's illustrations in the instructions, formed a multifaceted look for the characters.

The character design changing across different parts of the game lets players experience them with the distinctions Monet afforded with his *Water Lilies* series. A few years later, when the feature film *Final Fantasy VII: Advent Children* released, Square showed off how far their 3D animation had progressed. Between *Advent Children* and the lavishly modeled and animated video games *Final Fantasy VII: Remake* and *Rebirth*, the characters now have very specific looks. *Remake* and *Rebirth* are gorgeous, but I will admit something is lost with that amount of detail. I enjoyed filling in the details, projecting myself into the characters, and appreciating how stylish it all was. But now we can count Aerith's pores, so when **[REDACTED]** it packs a stronger emotional punch, I guess.

Since Impressionists were more interested in capturing vibes than in cataloging the world, the viewer needs to imagine those visual details and what their other senses would capture in the same place. If we aren't interacting with paintings that way, it's not fair to say we've seen it. To paraphrase David Lynch in regard to watching a movie on "your fucking telephone," you'll not have experienced it; you'll have experienced a "weakness" ("David Lynch"). Really, all art is interactive; the question is how it's interactive. The crux of games is that they offer feedback. That's their native language and where their interactivity finds its most meaning.

Pokémon Red and *Blue*, in case you aren't familiar, casts players as a prepubescent boy leaving home to explore the wonderful world of Pokémon (a portmanteau of "pocket monsters"). It's kind of a sci-fi Shintoism: players capture magical, element-aligned creatures in the pokéballs and train them to fight other people's Pokémon. I played the first generation of *Pokémon* games on my Game Boy Color, and one of the things that stood out to me was how the world as you experience it in the game doesn't make any sense. Yeah, it's a game about training sapient, animals to do combat through the fundamental forces of the universe, but that's what I signed up for. The second weirdest thing, for me, about the first generation of Pokémon games is how many buildings you can't enter. After that, it's how a society functions without knowing anything.

To start, Professor Oak tells you there are 150 Pokémon and SOMEHOW that's enough biodiversity to sustain a large island. And SOMEHOW people have not memorized everything there is to know about these critters, even though they power humans' everyday lives. Then again, how could they? The player character, a child, is tasked with catching all 150 Pokémon. Catching one generates its pokédex entry. Who writes the pokédex entries? Why hasn't Oak done this with any of the region's Pokémon masters? Why do you pass out and lose half your money if you lose a Pokémon battle? The answer is: shut up. It's a fun game for children.

Having played video games for as long as I can remember, I'm willing to accept these oddities. What struck me as odd was how many buildings I couldn't enter. Cities in *Pokémon's* Kanto region don't seem to have any grocery stores. Each fully loaded bookshelf contains one readable book. The science museum has the space shuttle *Columbia*. The implications of some of these are more bizarre than others.

Pokémon isn't about surviving in the wild, camping in forests and caves, rationing provisions, and the uncomfortable questions of the food chain. The game doesn't really care about food, let alone grocery stores. As for the books, it could be that the player character simply has no interest in anything that isn't related to Pokémon. It could also mean only books about Pokémon exist, which is a bit more dystopian. As for the space shuttle, maybe *Pokémon* is in a far future and people with space-bending technology look back fondly at the struggles of pre-Poké people. Maybe the developers just thought space is neat. Whichever way someone reads these details, if they consider them at all, is fine. There doesn't have to be a correct answer. The developers need only to give us the impression of a world. Interacting with these elements in the game world doesn't give the player any feedback; they aren't relevant to the rules, and they remind us that we're playing a game. Bizarre details serve as a splash of impressionistic color on the game's video.

This all outlines my thinking as I delve into two games I read as impressionistic art: *Lil Gator Game* and *Ryuutama*. I'm not saying these are the best, or even correct, artistic readings of these games. I wanted to relate games to Impressionism, and these two titles lend themselves rather nicely. And for our purposes, there are no "correct" ways of looking at art, only "more useful" and "less useful." I don't want to get too deep into Barthes' "Death of the Author" right now, so suffice to say audiences can read texts however they'd like (51). The credentials of the reader are nowhere near as important as how interesting the reading is, and a game where you play as a lil' gator is loam rich with meaning.

For readers already versed in game genre and marketing, both *Lil Gator Game* and *Ryuutama* fit snugly into the "cozy game" category. On the developer's website, *Lil Gator Game*'s genre is "wholesome adventure"

("Lil Gator Game"), while *Ryuutama* is subtitled "Natural Fantasy Role Play" (Okada). These might seem a little twee for serious artistic discussion, but even in Impressionism, there's an unfortunate history of writing off anything not suitably masculine and dramatic.

In the 1870s, "social custom continued to prevent bourgeois women from wandering the streets unaccompanied," so rather than paint favorite bars and cafés as male painters did, women were "confined to drawing on their personal experiences and perspectives in private boudoirs and the domestic sphere" (Hessel 111–112). Berthe Morisot's piece at the first Impressionist exhibition was a portrait of her sister; *The Cradle* portrays Edna Morisot gazing at her baby sleeping behind a muslin canopy and "seems to hint at the emotional complexities of being a mother." It was dismissed by critics as a "sweet painting of motherhood" (Hessel 113).

In games, this conversation sometimes takes the form of whether or not a given title is a game at all. Games such as *What Remains of Edith Finch* and *Gone Home* were decried as "walking simulators" devoid of any meaningful interactivity and dealt with "themes like race, class, identity, and so forth...they're *political*, which is which is just about the worst and most annoying thing a video game can be" (Singal). Some critics have gone so far as to criticize the politics and aesthetics of identifying with characters at all, pointing to games such as *SimCity* as the kind of abstracted system on which games should focus (Bogost). The question of whether or not a specific title is even a game because it's not about shooting guns or building a city is similar to asking what place a woman's work had in a gallery when it was just a nice painting of a mother and child. I should mention that these arguments can be in good faith: it's entirely fair to ask whether *Blippo+*, an alien television channel, is a game (Frushtick).

"Cozy games" have received the same kinds of criticism women's paintings and walking sims did before them. Some "people think cozy games are girl games," which is partly to say they're simple and easy, but that's "missing the point" (Tach). In my experience, "cozy" is more a mindset than it is a description of the game. A martial arts game I can play well without feeling too much demand relaxes me. *Sifu* on easy mode or *Street Fighter 6*'s training mode are chill rhythm games. On the other hand, I cannot play *Stardew Valley* because there is just *so much* to it. Some people find running a farm and building relationships with the valley's townspeople as a pleasant way to spend hundreds of hours. Not me: it's too much to keep in my head. Since cozy games are more about capturing a mood and a moment with varying degrees of conflict and drama, *Lil Gator Game* and *Ryuutama* are easier to read as Impressionistic. They are sweet games about playing, but they're also about how we find joy and pleasure as we move through the world, and even how tension between people is as natural as sunshine.

Lil Gator Game is what it says on the tin. It opens with the titular gator (I named mine "Tater Gator," which is how I will refer to the character) playing "Legend of Hero" at a park with their older sister. Tater plays the hero while their sister handles playing the monsters and narrating the adventure. Jumping a few years ahead, Tater Gator and their sister return to the park while she is on break from college. Tater Gator wants her to come play with them and their friends, but she's stuck on her laptop doing more than her fair share of the work in a group assignment. I've never seen anyone, especially a humanoid alligator, looking so morose on a swing.

Tater decides they need to get their sister to put down their "stupid" game development homework. (She didn't have the benefit of this book.) The best way to do that, obviously, is to make a new Legend of Hero live action role-playing game, one that is so fun no older sister could resist! Tater enlists the help of their friends and makes new friends to make a sprawling playground castle and cardboard cutout monsters. When their older sister sticks to her homework, Tater realizes that when they and their sister played together, Tater was playing, and their sister was doing the work of making a game.

Play in *Lil Gator Game* consists mostly of Tater running around the map's islands and finding people to play with. Generally, folks are wrapped up in some small drama, actual or playful, of their own, and Tater needs to resolve those before their friend pitches in. Progress, as much as it is meted out, is gated with goal milestones and not opening map locations or gaining character abilities. It reminds me how I felt meandering around Hyrule. As James Stephanie Sterling said in her review: "It takes place in a world where heroes are always clad in green and wear pointy hats, filled with monsters and stock fantasy characters in dire need of help. Best of all, it's a world entirely made up by children who are essentially playing a massive LARP."

Much of the game's charm comes from its look and sound. I'm not including *Lil Gator* because it looks like an Impressionist painting, but rather it looks one way an Impressionist game might. "The warm colours, paired with a bright sun and blue sky, make it incredibly cosy, and listening to water trickle by in streams and leaves rustle underfoot as I dash around is like being transported into the physical interpretation of a Headspace [a guided meditation app] soundscape" (Hefford). Players can even toggle between default cartoony graphics and a "chonky" mode. The "chonk" is not really the low polygon count and fuzzy textures of older games; it's more of a filter, making everything a bit pixelated. It looks the way people remember Nintendo 64 games looking, even if *Lil Gator Game* is much smoother. The game "balances the childlike veneer of the protagonist's perspective with a poignant emotional core that's reminiscent of [*The Legend of Zelda*] *Wind Waker*" (Diaz).

"[*Wind Waker*], like many Zelda games, has a somber story at its center, but it also features a cartoony, cel-shaded look and markedly whimsical dialogue and world design. Link fights monsters but also meets eccentric characters, like a man who dons an all-white fringe jacket and dances day and night and a group of school children who bully Link but then challenge him to hide-and-seek" (Diaz). If *Lil Gator*'s calling out to *Zelda* amounted just to feeling nice and looking like a GameCube title, it would be a charming, nostalgic little game. It impresses by tying these ideas to more complex feelings and remembrances for both the player and Tater Gator. Throughout the map, Tater stumbles across pastel-toned, younger versions of their sister and themselves and remembers what, in that moment, their sister taught them about growing up. They usually have a tongue-in-cheek tone, like when Tater climbs up real high and their sister congratulates them… before telling them not to tell anyone she let them climb so high.

By the time they find this memory, the player probably knows that big sis has nothing to worry about: this world does not have fall damage. Failing falling on their own, one of the NPCs tells Tater that they can safely drop from any height. To get one of the game's trophies (goals either part of or aside from regular gameplay), players limply drop ("ragdoll") until they hit terminal velocity. As the game's combat is Tater vs. cardboard monsters, falling is the only aspect of the game with any appearance of danger. Combined with Tater and their sister doing the work of game design in the game itself, *Lil Gator* invites players to think about what it is game designers actually, you know, *do*.

When I tell people I make games, they often ask, "Oh, so you're a programmer?" No, but I understand why people think that I must be. Video games look so little like traditional games and that obscures the fact that they are rules-based systems. When one of Monet's paintings from the 1877 *L'Impressionniste* exhibition was accused of being "merely pictures of places" and had no "possibility of reminiscence and reflection," Georges Rivière responded: "Looking at this magnificent painting, one is seized by the same emotion as before nature, and this emotion is perhaps stronger still, for in the painting there is that of the artist as well" (Broude 28). Art isn't about just what it's about, so it behooves the creators to work with their own perspectives and experiences. It's on us, the audience, to do the work of thinking about what this game, for instance, says about being young.

Playing *Lil Gator Game*, I remembered TV shows', movies', and my parents' stories about childhood. Cartoons would make wild promises of childhood adventures with actual, and sometimes deadly, stakes. Movies followed competent kids as they escaped the confines of their home or stood up to unjust peers in conflicts with emotional weight. My parents would have me believe that Beverly Cleary's novels and the less distressing parts of *To Kill a Mockingbird* were typical experiences. "We didn't go home until the streetlights came on," my parents would bemoan while telling me to go outside. And I did sometimes! But real life wasn't like *Stand by Me* or *My Side of the Mountain*. Those stories came from a mid-century mindset where children could adventure, scrape their knees, trespass, and generally get up to mischief, and they wouldn't be in the deepest of trouble. *Lil Gator Game*, with its sprawling game-in-a-game, led me to feel the way those stories told me I should have felt as a child. By being a game about games, *Lil Gator* got me thinking about the nature of my play as a child and how I was told I should feel about it. It isn't just a game that feels the way I remember *Ocarina of Time* feeling; it's a game that changed the way I feel remembering *Ocarina of Time*.

My favorite of *Lil Gator*'s nuts-and-bolts design elements is how it uses its quests to make exploration feel valuable. I'm not a huge fan of exploration for its own sake. I want some sort of systems benefit. If a location looks cool, but I don't get anything interesting for finding it (experience points don't cut it), I'm ambivalent. Even so, I'm not immune to a game world's sense of presence. Standing on top of *Lil Gator*'s radio tower and looking at the hazy reaches of trees and sea, I felt a bit of the enormity and potential of the space. Broude similarly describes Casper Friedrich's painting *Chalk Cliffs on Rügen* (Figure 2.1). "The human figures are still portentously dwarfed by the colossal forms of nature…Like them, we cling to the rocks in the foreground, in awe of the abyss below, separated physically by insurmountable spatial barriers from the vastness of the sea and the almost supernatural glow of the light-filled space beyond."

FIGURE 2.1 Casper Friedrich, *Chalk Cliffs on Rügen*, 1818, oil on canvas.

That sounds quite a bit like game exploration and speaks to how all artforms have the potential for meaningful interaction. *Lil Gator*'s design is so vital because its creators have a perspective on games and play. It's not just "something to say," though the game does say that the way we play when we're children has to change. The perspective is the creators' feelings evoked in players. It's melancholy, funny, purposeful, and sometimes frustrating. *Lil Gator Game* is a game about how we feel when we take control of our own play.

I'm fascinated by the ways tabletop roleplaying games blur the lines between designer and player. "Gamemasters" (GMs) is the generic term for the person who runs the game, plans play sessions, adjudicates rules, supports play, and generally keeps the whole adventure going. When GMing, it's usually good to think about the people at your table and what they want out of the game. That's about as bespoke as game design can get. But GMs are also players: they roll dice and sometimes talk in accents, and that's as playful as it gets. Party members, which is probably a better descriptor than "players," offer real-time feedback to GM choices not just by voicing what they like or don't like about the experience, but by making choices in the adventure. Following one thread or taking one action over another communicates to the GM similarly to how players would at a play test.

Sometimes, the roles are further blended when the GM has a player-style character of their own. I had a character of my own when I ran a *Witcher Tabletop RPG* campaign, mostly because I enjoy fighting monsters and hanging out with the party. There was also the practical benefit that in *The Witcher*, only the eponymous monster hunters do full damage to supernatural enemies. Much to my surprise at character creation, no one in my party wanted to play a witcher. More generally, DM-controlled heroes are often powerful allies who jump into a scene, do something cool, then take off for an adventure that fleshes out the world. *The Lord of the Rings*' Gandalf is a good equivalent, giving help and guiding quests when he is most needed. These kinds of character tools for the GM to maintain control over the campaign's plot. *Ryuutama*'s "ryuujin" is a different approach.

I haven't yet really defined "tabletop roleplaying game," and even with the cultural prevalence of *Dungeons & Dragons* in TV, movies, and podcasts, a lot of people don't have a good sense of what a roleplayer *does.* When I started playing *D&D* in college, I had a hard time wrapping my head around it. I had seen characters on TV play it, but anyone who's watched any TV show or movie about games knows that even if the game and show were made to sell each other, rules get bent in storytelling. When my first scenario (of course, it was in a tavern with a rat problem) was laid out, I asked a typical new player question: "What do I do?" The difficult thing for new RPG players is that the answer is a question: "What do you want to do?" *D&D* novices benefit from the game's pretty straightforward play loop, which is "kill enemies to get money, use money to get better stuff, use better stuff to kill stronger enemies." Repeat this process until your character is killed or has become a god. Other game systems are a bit more abstract or complex, but play looks about the same for most tabletop RPGs (TRPGs).

Usually, there is a table and a gamemaster. There are players. Players have character sheets they use to record their characters' abilities, equipment, and so on. The gamemaster will probably have planned dungeons, towns, NPCs, and whatnot. These plans will often prove useless, as players want to get up to mischief and will drop an adventure hook faster than a big-mouth bass.

When a player wants their character to do something at which they might fail, they roll a die. A lot of games use 20-sided (d20) or 10-sided (d10) dice for general "checks." Players add the number they rolled to any relevant character skills and equipment and tell the GM their total. If it ties with or is higher than the difficulty number set by the GM, the character succeeds. If it's lower, they fail, and someone else gets to try something. This is more or less how these games operate in and out of combat, though exceptions are varied and wild. Games might do something different with dice or use a different resolution system altogether.

Some games have players roll under, instead of over, target numbers to succeed; the better a character is at something, the higher their stat, the more likely they are to roll under their stat. It makes sense, though I enjoy "bigger number=good." Some systems—like the wildly popular "Powered by the Apocalypse" rule set/engine by D. Vincent Baker and Meguey Baker—use levels of success to push the story forward while deemphasizing tactical combat (Wieland). In *The Quiet Year*, players draw maps to "define the struggles of a community living after the collapse of civilization, and attempt to build something good within their quiet year. Every decision and every action is set against a backdrop of dwindling time and rising concern" (Avery). Some games, like *Star Crossed* and *Dread*, have players pull from balancing block towers rather than roll dice. I have a copy of *Jukebox: The Karaoke Musical Tabletop Roleplaying Game,* and I cannot wait to play it. That one doesn't have a GM. Neither do *Star Crossed* (which is 2-player) nor *The Quiet Year*. Oh, and *Quiet Year* doesn't really have individual characters, but players take on the roles of groups of people in a community. RPGs are an exciting and wild corner of the gaming landscape.

At first glance, *Ryuutama* looks more or less like *D&D*. The rulebook says, "...it's like an evolved version of *Candy Land*," which is as incorrect as anything that has ever been said about a game, but maybe I just don't appreciate *Candy Land* lore. Maybe what is meant is that players walk across a picturesque landscape, but *Candy Land* is actually a zero-player game, so a better description is necessary.

Ryuutama is affectionately called "Hayao Miyazaki's Oregon Trail," referring to the Japanese animation director of *My Neighbor Totoro* and *Spirited Away* fame (Rioja) and the educational game about a family of white, 19th-century colonizers moving West (Salgarolo). While both *Oregon Trail* and *Ryuutama* both put a lot of focus on resource management during long travels, the former is best known for characters dying of dysentery. *Ryuutama*'s rules do provide for characters getting food poisoning, but the diarrhea is never fatal. The comparison is more apt when you look at *Ryuutama* as a game "about journeys and helping people, not actually about fighting monsters" (Rioja). *Ryuutama* characters are not the god-killers of a *Dungeons & Dragons* party, with some critics going so far as to say the game "explores the lives of typical NPC's" (Manente). In this game, "Travelers" don't so much save the world as sustain it.

Ryuutama party members are called Travelers, craftspeople embarking on a naturalist, irreligious pilgrimage. In the game's setting, adults are "expected to leave their hometown for an extended journey at least once in their lifetime" and might start their journey for any reason, including simply feeling like it (Okada 14). This flexibility is a good way to get players invested during character creation. That process begins with choosing a Class, which is job-based and determines the character's skills. The classes are Minstrel, Merchant, Healer, Hunter, Artisan, Farmer, and Noble. *Ryuutama* is meant to initiate players into TRPGs, so some classes are recommended for new players, and others are for players with more experience. The class is then modified by picking a Type: attack (combat), technical (skilled problem solving), or magic (…magic). Then players assign roles within the party itself, which blurs the line between the character and their player.

The party roles are leader, mapper, quartermaster, and journal keeper. Each role has in-game and out-of-game aspects, for instance, the quartermaster character should have a pack animal, and their player keeps track of the party's rations (Okada 54–55). Travelers' journeys are not vacations. They aren't even breaks from the ordinary. *Ryuutama* is a game about everyday people plying their trades and giving rise to stories to harmonize the world. The harmonization is literal: ethereal dragons eat stories fed to them by Ryuujin (Okada 15).

"Ryuutama" is a portmanteau of the Japanese words for "dragon" and "egg." "Jin" is "person." As much as the game is about the Travelers, it is also about the Ryuujin tending to the dragons who embody the seasons.

> Seasonal dragons do not eat normal food, but instead consume "Travelogues", the very stories that are borne of those who traverse the world of Ryuutama. The Ryuujin record Travelogues from the deeds of Travelers and offer them to the seasonal dragons...And, as the seasonal dragons grow, the world, too, becomes brighter and more colorful. The form of the seasonal dragons, and of the world itself, depends on the type of travelogues consumed.
>
> (*OKADA 20*)

The Ryuujin themselves look like humans (beautiful humans, of course) with small wings on their heads and proportional wings on their backs (because anime). Their role reminds me less of a high fantasy mentor-type than of a patron god in Greek mythology. Each Ryuujin has a handful of Artefacts and Bénédiction spells (accents are the game's) to support compelling play, but not necessarily to support the Travelers. The Green Dragon Ryuujin can carry a torch Artefact which doubles the growth of Travelers, while the Black Dragon has a dagger that the GM can use to kill any NPC. Artefacts' varied uses let Ryuujin circumvent the rules a bit for better storytelling.

Conversely, Bénédiction is a mixed-diegesis spell. The Ryuujin has to spend resources to cast a Bénédiction, and that modifies play. There's a list of Bénédiction any Ryuujin can use to help or hinder Travelers, including rewinding or fast-forwarding time. There are also spells specific to each Ryuujin's dragon, which are more specific and help the players pursue the kind of story everyone at the table wants to tell. The Azure Dragon's "The Tale of the Heart" has players award each other tokens for roleplay that "moves someone's heart." The tokens can be traded to avoid the effects of dysentery. The Crimson Dragon's spells all focus on combat (Okada 136–146). By picking which dragon to feed, the players pick the type of story they'll tell.

While the GM is the narrator and adjudicator, the same as most RPGs, they also take an active and direct part in play. This includes the Ryuujin's creation and growth (they also get stronger) as well as managing their own magic components. Unlike in most games, where the GM can rule by fiat and not have to worry about their own in-game currency, the Ryuujin and Travelers all have to play basically the same way.

For setting expectations, the Traveler players, not the Ryuujin player, determine which dragon they want their adventure to feed. Regardless of which dragon they pick, the game operates fundamentally the same. This is partly due to how the Ryuujin relates to Travelers and partly because of the tone set by the rulebook. Mostly *Ryuutama* games follow a similar vibe because the rules are consistently interested in travel, not combat. If the focus of a campaign is the rain-soft Azure Dragon, the adventure will be gentler, but even a Crimson Dragon adventure with its more robust combat won't feel like *Dungeons & Dragons. D&D* is largely about tactics and treasure, so armor comes in various materials and styles, so players have to balance the amount of protection they want (e.g., half plate or full plate) with their class's abilities and statistical strengths. *Ryuutama* has four armors: "light, medium, heavy" and "clothes." In any of its flavors, *Ryuutama* is about the generation of memories. Players feel that process of generation through different moods.

One of the funniest things, to me, about the fine art viewing experience is how people are expected to "perform" looking. I tend to struggle with the ostensible purpose of going to see art. That is, experiencing and/or enjoying the art. I have the inclination to study and critique, to get something out of the museum visit or concert, rather than just take in the art. I'm trying to figure out how I can emulate or avoid artists' strategies, so I'm imagining them imagining me as an audience member. On top of that, I'm trying to look like a "good" audience member. I'm trying to be a good player in the art space. Similarly, people, who play games (especially video games), tend to try to play an RPG "right," instead of playfully.

By clearly laying out and dividing the responsibilities of play, *Ryuutama* balances "looked at-ness." Everyone knows how to be the "good" audience member engaging with the experience both as someone enjoying the game as well as someone helping other people enjoy it. Generally, RPGs are good for game designers to play because GMs have to consider how other people will react to their choices. *Ryuutama* gets everyone thinking that way, so even Travelers are invested in how the adventure moves through different environments.

One of the most powerful ways *Ryuutama* imparts a sense of place is the questionably named Minstrel class. Once per session, the Minstrel can learn a song from their current environment, either from the weather ("Rain Song") or the terrain ("Ballad of the Grassland"). These songs all do the same thing (other players get a +1 to their next roll) and can be played whenever the circumstances match the song (Okada 63). It gets players thinking about the *plein air* and the feeling of the ground underfoot. Reusing reminds Travelers change when adventurers aren't there, and learning songs encourages players to go to more kinds of places in all kinds of weather. It's the same kind of texturing one could expect from Impressionist paintings.

Ryuutama's approaches to place and space remind me of Monet's *Charing Cross Bridge* series. Monet's series reveals the "world as we actually see it: not a fixed, absolute perspective illusion in the eye of a frozen spectator within the limited frame of the picture window, but a thousand different glimpses of a constantly changing scene caught by a constantly moving eye" (Arnason 30). In *Charing Cross Bridge: Fog on the Thames*, 1903, the softening light refracts a steely blue on the water's surface ("Charing Cross Bridge") (Figure 2.2).

FIGURE 2.2 Claude Monet, *Charing Cross Bridge: Fog on the Thames*, 1903, oil on canvas.

Charing Cross Bridge on the Thames, c. 1903, hanging in the Saint Louis Museum of art is a very different example of the "thousand glimpses": the brush stroke sky is a sparse turmeric, and the river reflects it and a train as it crosses the bridge. London's skyline is hazy in the background, still steely but outlined in a soft blue ("Charing Cross in London"). It's not hard to imagine Travelers in either of these settings, the Minstrel learning "Foggy Shanty" or "Sun's Hymn" (Figure 2.3).

FIGURE 2.3 Claude Monet, *Charing Cross Bridge in London*, 1903, oil on canvas.

The crux of an impression is that forming one, even though it feels automatic, is something our brains *do*. It's not play, but it is an effort we put forth similar to how we play games. Impressions and snap judgments are foundational considerations of interface and experience design, but *Lil Gator Game* and *Ryuutama* use impressions to improve and better understand play. We can apply the same kind of Impressionist impulses to what we make and give players a feeling of what a place can mean. Understanding games this way can help us reflect not only how it's fun to interact with an environment or a character, but also how to remind players of sensations from their own lives. The more we give players an impression of feelings, the more they're invited to reflect on them and enjoy their play even after the fact. A post-impression, if you will.

Detroit-based educator Neil Jones wanted to make a video game, so that's what he learned how to do. In 2021, he released *Never Yield*, a "narrative runner" about making your way across the city as stylishly as possible. Since then, under the *nom de jouer* Aerial_Knight, he has released several games, including his newest title, *Dropshot*, an FPS literally about racing to the bottom. Seriously, it's a skydiving game where you play as a guy who was "bitten by a radioactive dragon." (Dropshot) Awesome.

I sat down with Neil and talked a bit about his experience being an independent artist in games.

B: I guess to start, tell us, tell us a bit about your work and how you got started making games.

A_K: Yeah. So, my name is Neil Jones. I go by Ariel_Knight online. I guess you would call that my artistic name and all that. But, you know, regular story of a kid who was a homebody, nerdy, whatever. Video games were my way to escape and all that. That's pretty much every gamer's story. And most game developers' stories.

But where I kind of stand out a little bit, after high school, I didn't really know what I wanted to do, and I saw those crappy commercials about making video games, and I went to one of those terrible trade schools. But it did open my eyes to the fact that I could do game development, that it was a real thing. It wasn't magic or anything like that. And I have a really addictive personality. So once I learned 3D art, I was like, addicted to it for like 4 or 5 years and got really good at it.

And then I picked up some more skills and more skills, but couldn't find placement in the game industry. It was very much a young industry and a boys' club of specific types of people or whatever, so it wasn't really open to different types of people at that time. So that's where a lot of people stopped, and I just kind of gave myself a chance. I was fortunate enough to have a support system where I could take some time off work and kind of work on my own thing. And I took advantage of that to kind of make my own game.

It came out during COVID and during a rough time in the world where a story about a black character kind of running through the streets and causing chaos without murdering everything was something that people were looking for at the time. And, you know, people liked it, so I kind of just kept going with it. And that's where I'm at now, where we have three games. This [*Dropshot*] would be the fourth game coming out and working on a couple more. You know, we don't make really big games, AAA games or anything like that, but we have a really specific audience, and we're trying to grow that audience and make things that more people will enjoy, that'll get my message across.

We kind of expand every now and then to be a little bit bigger and a little bit bigger. And I think we're successfully doing that. I'm getting better at making games as well as getting more used to the process. So, yeah, that's kind of a really, really condensed version of, you know, the last 15, 20 years.

B: That's fantastic. Talk to me a little bit about your audience. How did how did you find them? How did they find your games? And how do you continue to think of and relate to them?

A_K: Yeah. So, you know, these are all assumptions. I can just kind of take it from what I experienced of the people I've met who enjoy the things that I make. And I think my audience is people who love video games, who look for different experiences, not just the standard AAA things. It's mostly people who just really like the form of video games and want to hear from different people making different things because my games feel different from other people's games because I have a different message. I have a different background. And the style of my games is a little bit different than most.

So I think that's kind of where my audience starts from. But now, people who like creative and different games that are a bit smaller so they don't have to spend 100 hours trying to play one game, they can play something really unique, really quick, and support a creator who's trying to just make his own space in the industry. The audience is slowly growing. I think we're including more people who are interested in game development as a whole, and they want to watch our process and see how we can get a game out in one year and have all the bells and whistles. And then that's why we use Discord to talk to people and just kind of post the whole process. That's been going really well. You know, it's not the biggest thing in the world, but, you know, people enjoy it.

B: I've seen the Discord and Patreon communities are pretty thriving. That's really impressive. Talking a bit about something I talk to my students about a lot: you don't necessarily want to create anything truly original, because then no one will know what to do with it. People won't know how to talk about it or market it. How do you balance your games being specific and unique with how to talk about them with people?

A_K: So the *Never Yield* games were my take on a runner. You know, people weren't really interested in runners when I first made the game. But it actually has an ending, it has smooth jazz, it has cutscenes with a story, and how we twisted the gameplay at the end. People were like, "This is really different for a runner."

Dropshot is my take on a shooter because I never wanted to make a shooter. Putting a gun in somebody's hand and being, like, "shoot that," isn't the most interesting to me. But how about he shoots stuff without a gun? His whole backstory is he got bitten by a radioactive dragon and now he can do weird stuff, you know? And there's a cow who gives him powers.

So this is weird, different, creative take on standard gameplay. We're working on a puzzle game now that's really different from most puzzle games. It's like my take on a puzzle. You take that base core game mechanic and then you add something to it, and then you say, "What if this?" to kind of twist it up and make people interested in it because a normal shooter isn't interesting.

It's the branding that people buy now, not the gameplay. With my games, it's the gameplay. People aren't checking out the branding as much.

B: Could you talk good about your influences, both from other games and then from outside of games?

A_K: Yeah. My biggest two influences are *No More Heroes* by Suda51 [Goichi Suda] because it's just a wild game and you play that, you can definitely feel the humor and personality of the people who made it. It's so unique. And it does some wild stuff that, you know, I would probably never do in a game and other people would never do, but that specific team was like, "Yeah, we rock with this."

And then *Persona 5*. People really sleep on *Persona 5*, but I think it really changed the game industry with how much style you can add into a game. And how the boring daily life stuff really matters when [a player is] trying to relax, and then when you're trying to be intense, it's a little bit of everything. Anybody can get some enjoyment out of that game. It was like a different take on an RPG, mixed with a light novel type of game. So I think I draw most of my inspirations from those two games. And because they kind of match my natural art style, I can use them to help direct myself. But I also don't want to limit myself into just those things. I try to find ways to kind of break out and update certain things and kind of just be really different.

B: How about from outside of games? Where do you find yourself going for inspiration? And those updates you were talking about?

A_K: Oh man. It's more of the feel of anime. People say, "Oh, what kind of anime?" It's the feel of it, you know? There's certain anime that make you feel a certain way. *My Hero Academia* makes you feel inspired and that you can be anything you want to be. And then, there's games that make you feel really, really sad. Or anime that make you root for the villain.

I try to get those feelings from other forms like anime and movies and things like that. But yeah, I try to make what I know as well. So I pull from anime and superhero movies and things like that, and try to keep that, that vibe anytime I'm about to do an animation. There are really specific anime that I watch because I want to have that momentum going into what I'm going to make.

B: Could you talk about a specific instance of doing that?

A_K: Yeah. So for *We Never Yield*, I really wanted my animations to have impact, so I studied the impact frames from anime and poured those into it and learned how to do impact frames. My impact frames are terrible. So I had this really good friend who draws a lot, and she never did impact frames either, but she had more time to work on it. So I did a first pass, and then she did the second pass, and we both were happy with it, and we came together with a third and fourth pass that was like, "Okay, this is the workflow."

We had to kind of come up with a workflow. We thought would be like one image, but it needs to be two or three images to really hit and show movement. So, you know, that's a good example of me pulling from anime to kind of add to what I already do.

B: Talking a bit about that, what does your team look like now? Is that friend of yours still working on the games at all? How's that going these days?

A_K: So, yeah, different for now. She just kind of does comic book stuff, she wasn't ever really into games too much. My team is pretty much me and three coders because coding was the weakest part of my skill set. I could do it here and there and do enough to kind of get things set up, but I need three coders now to help me. Like one, specifically, just for all the weird menus that I make. And one for all the cutscenes to make sure everything flows between gameplay and cutscenes. And then one purely for gameplay. Once somebody is done, they move on to the next project, and I'm just doing art between two projects the entire time, like the cutscenes, the promotional art, the animations, tweaking the gameplay and creating the gameplay. So we have a good four-person team right now, and I'm trying to keep it to that. It's sort of a very technical, collaborative relationship.

B: I know you are very forward on playtesting, taking feedback, and integrating it. Could you talk a bit about how you maintain what you want your game to be while still being collaborative and taking feedback from anyone you get to play your game?

A_K: Yeah. So we talk about feedback a lot. And this is a dictatorship. I tell people that all the time. These are my games, my vision, my name is on them. It is a collaborative process, but there is something really special about one person's vision and people who support that. So, you know, the game I want to make, I pitch to my team and make sure everybody likes it.

Nine times out of ten, they're like, "That's amazing." They might say, "Oh, well, what if this? What if that?" And I'm totally open to all of those types of feedback and critique. But if the game's good, if it's bad, I want it to be my fault. I don't want it to be somebody else's idea or to be able to blame this person, to blame that person. Final decision is always mine. So even if someone does say, "Hey, we should do this," it was because I said, "Yes, I agree with that idea." So no matter what, it's always on me. It's more of me controlling my own destiny, that type of thing. And no one ever feeling bad for if something goes wrong or whatever: it's my fault, right?

With that said, you know, when we get feedback or anything like that, you have to kind of listen to the feedback and find out what the real problem is and not what they say. You know, some people are just mean, but even mean comments have a good point buried in there somewhere. You have to kind of pull that out. And even within the team, when they have certain feedback, "I don't like this about the game," I say, "Well, what don't you like? What, specifically, are we talking about?" And it's not even that thing most of the time, it's either a vibe or a feeling about where this or that pops up in the game. It's not that they don't like it; it's just that they don't like where it is.

There's a lot of talking involved and a lot of finding out how people really feel about certain things. And a little bit of therapy with people when they say they don't like this or that. That's in the team and outside of the team. Reading comments, I'm trying to, like, dissect what the real problem is.

B: This came up in another interview [with *System Mastery*]. There's more of a codified language around novels or movies or that kind of thing. Do you feel as though we have developed enough language to figure out what someone really has in mind? Do you ever bump up against this? How much of it is vibes and how we haven't agreed on what, you know, what certain words mean?

A_K: Yeah, it's more about vibes and consistency. My thing is, if one person says something that really doesn't matter. If three people say something is definitely a thing, and you have to figure out what's consistent throughout all of those comments. We talk about how games are an international thing, so it's really hard to have a specific language set for it.

And our industry is very, very young. It's not like we have too many real standards that have been around for a long time. I think where games are is where we're going to settle in for a while, with the graphics and how games work and the platforms and things like that. I think the more universal things become, the easier it's going to be to talk about these things.

But I think the biggest problem is that a lot of games aren't for a lot of people. For instance, I don't particularly like puzzle games as much. So if someone who doesn't like a certain type of game makes comments about not liking that game, you don't know that's not their genre, but they are trying to critique it. They're inherently not going to like it. So you have to take their feedback in a different way.

B: What made you want to make a puzzle game, if you don't like them as much?

A_K: Something different. I made a shooter, I made a runner. I made some story games. So I was like, "I can make a puzzle." And I had a really good idea. I was like, "Oh, man, I would play a puzzle game with a really creepy story. This is dope idea." So something different, something quick.

B: What's it been like for you being an independent artist, self-publishing? Especially, what's it like going to events like GDC [the Game Developers' Conference] where you have a cross-section of the entire field, internationally, there?

A_K: I mean, GDC is a lot chiller than people who haven't been think. The people who have been only a couple times think that it's intense because you're really forced to talk to people. But the whole going to events, it's just you forcing yourself to talk to people. You have to know your purpose for those events. If you're showing a game, you need to have your game on you and show it to everybody you can within that time frame. A lot of times I'm only in town for like two or three days, and I try to maximize that time as much as possible. As soon as I get off the plane, go drop off my stuff and go into like the cocktail hour or dinner or whatever and just trying to find out how I can push myself forward in the industry.

It can be overwhelming, especially when you don't know anybody, or you're just kind of showing up to a random event to kind of just be like, "I'm here." That's the first step: just kind of go into the thing. That's the biggest kind of block that you can run into.

But, I like to find the people who are in my range. So if I had been making games for just one year, I find other new people who are trying to make their first game and talk to them, because you have more alignment with them than a CEO or somebody who's been around for 20 years. You don't have as much to talk to them about, or they don't have as much reason to talk to you. I'm sure they would love to talk to you. But at the same time, you pick their brain, move on to the people who can directly help you more.

B: What surprised you in making your first game? And then what's the most recent surprise you've had for making a game?

A_K: Publishers, man. Publishers are extremely shitty. I never thought I would know the depths of how much I could come to hate a certain type of person in the industry. You know, there are good publishers, I've heard, but, the concept of publishers, not very good when you break it down. You look at it from like, a, a thousand miles away: they get a giant portion of your game for a loan. And then when you pay the loan back, they still get to keep taking a giant portion of your game.

I've just heard a lot of horror stories about publishers. It's not the people who work at publishing places. It's just the concept as a whole is something that really surprised me and bothered me. So I do my best to kind of warn people about it and avoid it myself. But I don't know, maybe I'll get a good publisher one day.

You end up doing a lot of the work that publishers are supposed to be doing. I do a lot of marketing. I'm out here a lot.

B: You said the field has sort of settled for a while. Where would you like to see games go in the next 5 or 10 years?

A_K: You know, I want gamers to appreciate the games more because games are very hard to make. And there are so many of them right now that it's really easy to not appreciate them or the people who make them. But you see a lot of studios closing. You see, you know, a lot fewer games being started. I think we're going to hit a drought one day, and then gamers are going to be like, "Oh, man, we really had a good with all these start ups and indies and whatnot."

Now we only have like ten releases under one publisher that owns everybody. Kind of like the movie industry. I think the game industry follows the movie industry, very closely, historically, but a lot quicker. If you look at the 100 years of movies, we're like in the year 40 already.

I think it's all up to the gamers and what they support and what they allow to happen. That's coming next. I just kind of hope we keep small games. I hope people keep their jobs, because people get replaced all the time. It's rough out here; you scroll through LinkedIn, you see everybody losing their jobs. And gamers are like, "Yeah! Where's the next trailer for Call of Duty 27?"

B: Then what advice would you give to someone? What's something you wish someone had told you when you started?

A_K: Yeah. The advice thing is weird. I don't give advice because, I always tell people, I came into this almost 20 years ago now. That was a completely different situation. You got to kind of make your own moves and just figure it out because everybody's path is different. But something I wish someone told me was, "Starting off on your own, everything that you make and everything that you do, make it something that you can reuse." Because I spent years making assets that I can't use anymore. That they were for art tests or whatever. As you make things, build up your library, make sure you organize your history of your work and have all that stuff backed up. I lost a lot of stuff that I could probably use or reuse now that I did early on.

BIBLIOGRAPHY

Alder, Avery, and Ariel Norris. *The Quiet Year: A Map-Drawing Game*. Buried Without Ceremony, United States, 2019.

Arnason, H. H. *History of Modern Art: Newly Revised and Enlarged Edition*. Harry N. Abrams, Inc. New York, 1977

Barmore, Nathaniel, and Ravachol, Epidiah. *Dread*. The Impossible Dream, United States, 2005.

Barthes, Roland. "Death of the Author." *The Rustle of Language*, Hill and Wang, New York, New York, 1986, pp. 49–55.

Broude, Norma. *Impressionism: A Feminist Reading*. Rizzoli. New York, 1991.

Bogost, Ian. "Video Games Are Better without Characters." The Atlantic, Atlantic Media Company, 13 Mar. 2015, www.theatlantic.com/technology/archive/2015/03/video-games-are-better-without-characters/387556/.

"Charing Cross Bridge." Saint Louis Art Museum, 6 Sept. 2025, www.slam.org/collection/objects/2727/.

"Charing-Cross Bridge in London: Claude Monet: | Collection." The National Museum of Western Art, Tokyo, 14 Jan. 2026, collection.nmwa.go.jp/en/P.1959-0154.html.

ConcernedApe. "Stardew Valley." 2016.

"David Lynch on iPhones - Full Clip." YouTube, Sir Mix-A-Lot Rare Music, www.youtube.com/watch?v=OQiQk8AJ0YI. Accessed 5 Apr. 2026.

Del Toro, Guillermo. "Frankenstein." Netflix, 2025.

Deren, Maya. "Meshes of the Afternoon." 1943

Diaz, Ana. "Lil Gator Game is the Zelda-like I didn't know I needed." Polygon, 16 April 2023.

"Dropshot (Press)." AERIAL_KNIGHT, www.aerialknight.com/dropshot-press.html. Accessed 18 Jan. 2026.

Frushtick, Russ, McElroy, Griffin, McElroy, Justin, and Plante, Chris. "The Besties Best Game Bracket: 2025 Edition, Part 2." *The Besties*. 26 December 2025.

Fujiwara, Lyla McBeath. "Jukebox: The Karaoke Musical Tabletop Roleplaying Game." Jar of Eyes Games, 2004.

Hefford, Hayden. "Lil Gator Game review: a heartfelt adventure about childhood antics." Rock Paper Shotgun, 15 December 2022.

"Interview with Shigeru Miyamoto." Miyamoto Shrine: Shigeru Miyamoto's Home on the Web, Nintendo Power, web.archive.org/web/20040619165414/www.miyamotoshrine.com/theman/interviews/111998.shtml. Accessed 4 Apr. 2026.

Guanzhong, Luo, and Martin Palmer (translator). "The Romance of the Three Kingdoms." Penguin Classics, 2018.

Layani, Jordan. "Sifu." Sloclap, Kepler Interactive, 2022.

"Lil Gator Game." Playtonic Games, 7 Jan. 2025, www.playtonicgames.com/game/lil-gator-game/.

MegaWobble. "Lil Gator Game." Playtonic Games, 2022.

Mello-Klein, Cody. "The Legend of Zelda: Tears of the Kingdom Is One of the Most Anticipated Games in Years. Almost 40 Years in, Why Is Nintendo's Hit Game Series Still so Popular?" Northeastern Global News, 3 May 2023, news.northeastern.edu/2023/05/03/zelda-tears-of-the-kingdom/.

Manente, Kristina. "Beyond D&D: The 12 Ttrpgs You're Not Playing, but Really Should Be." SYFY, SYFY, 26 Sept. 2024, www.syfy.com/syfy-wire/ttrpgs-board-games-rpgs-quiet-year-roleplaying-recommendations.

Miyamoto, Shigeru. "The Legend of Zelda: The Ocarina of Time." Nintendo 64, Nintendo, 1998.

Okada, Atsuhiro, and Ayako Nagamori. Ryuutama: Natural Fantasy RPG. Kyotodama Heavy Industries, 2017.

Rioja, Tomas Gimenez. "My Experience with Ryuutama (Why You Should Try It!)." Gnome Stew, 20 Nov. 2024, gnomestew.com/my-experience-with-ryuutama-why-you-should-try-it/.

Roberts, Alex. "Star Crossed." Bully Pulpit Games, 2019.

"Ryuutama: Natural Fantasy RPG." Ryuutama Natural Fantasy RPG, kotohi.com/ryuutama/. Accessed 29 Dec. 2025.

Salgarolo, Michael. "10 Facts about the Oregon Trail." Mental Floss, Mental Floss, 17 July 2020, www.mentalfloss.com/history/oregon-trail-facts.

Shelley, Mary. "Frankenstein; or, The Modern Prometheus." Penguin Classics, 2003.

Singal, Jesse. "Why the Video-Game Culture Wars Won't Die, Two Years after Gamergate." Intelligencer, 30 Sept. 2016, nymag.com/intelligencer/2016/09/why-the-video-game-culture-wars-wont-die-two-years-later.html.

Sterling, James Stephanie. "Lil Gator Game - Hijinks to the Past (Review)." The Jimquisition, 7 Jan. 2023, www.thejimquisition.com/post/lil-gator-game-hijinks-to-the-past-review.

Tach, Dave. "The Rise of Cozy Games." Epic Games Store, 24 Nov. 2025, store.epicgames.com/en-US/news/best-cozy-games-why-cozy-feature-interview.

Tajiri, Satoshi. Pokémon *Red, Blue, and Yellow.* Nintendo, 1998.

Whale, James. *Frankenstein.* Universal Studios, 1931.

Wieland, Rob. "A Beginner's Guide to Powered by the Apocalypse Games." Forbes, 29 Dec. 2019, www.forbes.com/sites/robwieland/2020/12/29/a-beginners-guide-to-powered-by-the-apocalypse-games/.

CHAPTER 3

Cult of Borderline Personality

Auteur Theory and Games

Are you ready to learn some more French? Of course you are. You are intelligent and cosmopolitan. But when *auteur theory* came for me, a bewildered film school student, I was wholly unprepared. Auteur theory is the idea that movies are authored by the director's singular, overriding voice. People riff on this theme, but the gist is that a film can be understood as the product of a single genius's… genius. This is an easier sell with art cinema where one person comes up with the scenario, operates the camera, edits the footage, maybe they even star in it. If you watch *Tetsuo: The Iron Man*, you'll know it has to be one person's vision because it hurts too much to imagine anyone else getting a say and that movie being the end result. I recommend it.

The Auteur is a harder argument to make with larger films, especially Hollywood movies. For one thing, directing might be the person's sole job. Not that it isn't enough job! It's just that a director has a bit more control when they're also the writer, producer, etc. Even if the director has all those positions, they still have to collaborate. There are actors, costumers, the cinematographer, and so many other people who contribute to a movie. Honestly, it's amazing any of these things ever come together, let alone maintain an identifiable style across one director's body of work,

DOI: 10.1201/9781003755821-3

but that's the argument first mounted by the critics for the 1950s French movie magazine *Cahiers* (Bordwell 81). It was their assertion that a film is *best* understood as the product of a brilliant mind, a sort of equivalent to literature's biographical criticism, and eventually auteurists argued "masterpieces are outside time and place" (Bordwell 81). I doubt it. I am not a fifth dimensional being and am still able to perceive art. Maybe I've just never seen a masterpiece.

Despite Hollywood's tumult and the insistence that video games are the current predominant medium, cinema is still a vital art form and hugely influential on video and tabletop games, so a working understanding of recent film history is useful for game makers. 1975's *Jaws* and 1977's *Star Wars*, early films from auteurs Steven Spielberg and George Lucas, started the trend which would become the summer blockbuster as we know it today (Morris). Spielberg and Lucas both had identifiable styles and interests and made successful movies, eventually becoming household names. Both movies started franchises, but Spielberg gave up control of *Jaws* decades before Lucas sold *Star Wars* to Disney. No matter what one thinks of the various *Star Wars* from *Episode I* on, *Jaws: The Revenge* originated the tagline-come-punch line "This Time It's Personal" (Klimek).

Eventually, Hollywood recruited auteur directors to work within existing (and I hate this term) intellectual properties. That's what people mean by "IP," if you've heard it repeated ad naseum but never defined. Auteurs' style has always been used to draw people to theaters. Alfred Hitchcock is a good example: if someone wanted a tense movie riddled with voyeuristic sexual metaphors, he was your man. Between his movies and TV show, Hitchcock *was* the brand. In the case of *Batman*, Tim Burton was hired because his Gothic, cartoonish aesthetic fit the character. It has a definite style, but still had wide enough appeal to gross over $400 million worldwide ("Batman").

In the decades since *Batman '89*, as it's colloquially called, the role of an auteur filmmaker has increasingly been to make a movie recognizably their own within an established (sigh) IP. Christopher Nolan's *The Dark Knight*, Guillermo del Toro's *Hellboy 2: The Golden Army* and *Blade II*, and Denis Villeneuve's *Blade Runner 2049* and *Dune* series are all excellent examples of auteurs making space for their voices within IP while turning in movies extant fans enjoy. In several of these instances, especially the del Toro films I mentioned, the director's voice could overtake what would make a movie fit nicely into a franchise. Of course *Blade II* has vampires whose jaws split in two directions; Guillermo del Toro always needs a more monstrous monster. A similar preoccupation is the driving force of David Lynch's *Dune* (1984), a movie made with no interest in its story but very interested in goopy creatures.

The idea of the auteur director is entangled with movie studios' marketing strategies. Critic Kristin Thompson asked herself how "prestige horror" films became a *thing* and found the studio itself, A24, is an "auteur." It's a great observation, and I have to agree. Thompson points out that the studio has fans of its own, people happy to buy soundtracks on artfully printed vinyl records and who follow the company's social media accounts. It makes sense. No matter how different two A24 movies are, they play in the same key. For my part, more than a few times, I've:

- seen a trailer, thought "I want to see that," and found out it was an A24 film
- been incredulous about a movie until I saw it was produced by A24
- gifted one of their neat Blu ray editions.

Authorship in video games is usually a bit closer to A24's branding strategy. Growing up, I knew Square, now Square Enix, made stylish fantasy roleplaying games. I could expect sweeping adventures with gorgeous soundtracks. Capcom made games that seemed straightforward in their genre (e.g., sci-fi, martial arts, zombie) and the play itself would be, even as the stories got wildly convoluted. Nintendo made games that felt like visiting a playground.

I'm not sure why people haven't subjected games to auteur theory as rigorously as they have movies, but I have my guesses. One reason is that academics and critics have only recently gotten interested in games as authored texts. Books like 1938's *Homo Ludens* were much more interested in play from an anthropological perspective and exploring how structured effort outside of labor creates meaning. For instance, religious ceremony and liturgy do not create anything material, but it is play that acts upon the spirit (Huizinga 18). Actual college courses studying games as authored works are fairly recent, which makes sense considering that *Super Mario Bros.* released in 1985 and it is only since then that people have made analog or video games with artistic aspirations.

As for criticism and review, early games journalists were more focused on a game being worth a player's time and money than they were interested in finding, or creating, meaning in a game. Given player demographics, that makes sense. According to the Interactive Digital Software Association's 1999 State of the Industry Report, "One of the most persistent myths in the world of video and computer games is that kids are the dominant audience. In fact, surveys show that the market for interactive games is much broader. The IDSA's 1998 Interactive Entertainment Attitude and Usage study revealed that 69 percent of those most frequently playing computer games and more than half (54 percent) of those most frequently playing video games are 18 years old or older" ("1999" 5). Adolescents weren't *Cahiers*' target demo. By comparison, in 2025, the average age of a video game player was 36 ("Annual ESA Study"). We now have a more adult audience interested in the people who make games.

Part of why I'm pushing for applying auteur theory to games is that it can be kind of fun to look into an artist's life and see how their work came about. I don't subscribe to the idea that great artists need to be very special and tortured geniuses, and it's called art*work* because they're working through their trauma. It's just that behind-the-scenes stories can be really interesting. But don't take my word for it: the *Community* episode "Documentary Filmmaking: Redux" has an argument as to whether the making-of documentary *Hearts of Darkness* is "way better" than *Apocalypse Now.* While I disagree on the ranking, *Hearts of Darkness: A Filmmaker's Apocalypse* adds a lot of depth to *Apocalypse Now* and tells the story of a production that basically "method acted" a war. You also get to see Marlon Brando accidentally swallow a bug.

It can also be fun to see an artist play with the same ideas in different pieces and to follow how their work changes over time. I'm always interested when an artist's obsessions override their better judgment. Nothing says director at work" like putting a barely disguised sexual fetish on screen. To which director am I referring? Take your pick! I don't want to get too into the weeds talking about how some of my favorite artists evolved in their ideas and execution, but I'm fascinated by seeing different approaches to themes like the cruelty of children or technical aspects like sound design. Watching someone experiment, change their mind, switch to something different, it gets me thinking about the effectiveness of ideas and how we communicate them.

For designers and developers, that's the best reason to apply auteur theory to games: it's a great way to learn how to make something that's consummately you. Emulating an artist you admire will take you only so far, though borrowing approaches and techniques is a good way to find your own style. It's more fundamental to look at how artists have leveraged their interests into making more textured work, or how they've pursued particular ideas, and emulate that kind of pursuit. The downside of all this is that auteurism easily turns into a cult of personality.

It's one thing if someone's fixation is, say, "Bardolatry." Loving Shakespeare too much is pretty inoffensive, him being dead and all. That said, if you've ever taken a film class, you likely know who some of the problematic living filmmakers are. No matter how many you have in mind, there are probably more! People's adoration has led to them defending all manner of literal crimes. In my case, a professor told us Roman Polanski should be allowed back in the US without fear of arrest for drugging and raping a 13-year-old girl. A lot of times, "genius" gets conflated with "being a monster," so while it's true that heinous people have made some truly great art, and we can learn a lot from those works, that kind of adoration is tacit permission to abuse people. There are ways to demand the best from oneself and collaborators without tormenting them.

For people who work in or play video games, working conditions can get especially thorny. For instance, it's generally known that game makers often face "crunch," which doesn't sound so bad. "Crunch" is the sound of candy bars and breakfast cereals. Anyway, people also call crunch "the death march" (Groen). Between those working conditions and the likelihood of getting laid off—33% of US and 28% of international respondents reported they'd been laid off in the past two years—it makes sense that 82% of the (US-based) industry supports unionization (Elderkin). As you might expect, studios have not been as open to the idea. Rockstar, which makes the *Grand Theft Auto* and *Red Dead* series, fired about 31 employees for what the studio claims was "gross misconduct." The employees say they were fired for trying to unionize (Webb).

Since I teach games, there's a certain sense of obligation to play *Grand Theft Auto VI* if, in fact, it is ever released. I'll have students who want to talk about the game, and if I say I'm not interested, I *guarantee* they'll tell me how good this one is. And it might be. I haven't played a *GTA* in a long time, but I fondly recall murdering a small nation's worth of *Vice City* dwellers. I'd be more worried about it if I couldn't borrow *GTA VI* from a library or read enough reviews to get a working knowledge, but it's still an ethical question I have to answer. The concern is more immediate for games journalists who have to play a game. I can just affect insouciance because I have the luxury of "voting with my dollar" or lack thereof.

Cultural labor necessarily intersects with artist and audience ethics. There are problems in every industry, but it's up to people who play games to spend our money as ethically as we can. That might mean passing up the occasional AAA game, but I'd argue that's no great hardship since there are so, so many good indie games. Bonus: if an indie game maker turns out to be an awful person, your money has more of an impact than it would on a corporate shareholder. The same holds true if they're personally decent and make cool games. For video games, indie games are a great venue to meaningfully interact with designers.

For tabletop games, the most important festival and award is Germany's Spiel des Jahres, or "Game of the Year." There's German efficiency for you. The most significant winner of the award and the progenitor of designer board games is Klaus Teuber's *Settlers of Catan*. It's the opinion of Rio Grande Games founder Jay Tummelson that Spiel Des Jahres pushed the craft of board games forward to differentiate American and European styles: *Catan* was the breakthrough "German-style" game (Green). As a side note, the documentary features interviews with Teuber and other leaders in the field, and they all pronounce it "kuh-tahn," not "kuh-taan." If you haven't played the game, it's probably about what you're imagining. Players compete to best develop an island by harvesting its resources (clay, wood, wool, wheat, and ore) to build roads and towns. It also has a desert where a robber lives. Presumably, the robber was on the island and chose to live in the desert rather than in a nice field or forest because robbers live in deserts.

Unlike board games with player elimination and direct conflict, no one gets knocked out of *Catan*. The closest thing to direct conflict is a player sending the robber to another player's resource well. It's a game driven by economics, chance, and positive feedback loops. It's easy enough to understand and has enough variability to welcome players with different levels of experience and interest in board games, which makes it a good game night choice for friends and families. And the concept is flexible enough to set historically, wrap in different IP (*Star Trek* and *Game of Thrones*), or adapt into other kinds of tabletop games ("Ludography"). Teuber's is the most successful European board game since Hnefatafl.

When I was in film school, the go-to example of an auteur was Alfred Hitchcock. His large body of work lends itself well to reading, rereading, and too-close reading. This is partly because his films are meticulously crafted, but it's also because Hitchcock was a weird guy and that's easy to see in his work. As our professors told us, Hitchcock's obsession with voyeurism and sex came from his strict Catholic upbringing. When he was a child, his father had him jailed for a night just to put the fear of god in him and that manifested later when he drilled peep holes in actresses' dressing rooms. Now, how much of that is true? I never checked and it doesn't matter. The point is that biographical anecdotes, no matter how apocryphal, are supposed to unlock the truth of how genius happens. If I seem ambivalent to this kind of thinking, that's my distaste for bowing to "genius" (see Chapter 1). Maybe it's a fool's errand for me to attempt excising fetishism from auteurism, but this can be a fun and useful way to look at work. Mostly, I'm put off by hero worship.

Luckily for me and my argument, Teuber's official biography has a feeling of pulling back the curtain on a great person's life to reveal the genesis of their greatness. His isn't as hagiographic as so many filmmakers' (there's not even any violence against women!), so the official bio is actually pretty charming:

> Klaus Teuber was born in 1952 at the foot of Breuberg Castle in the village of Rai-Breitenbach, surrounded by forests and gentle mountains. Did this rural, idyllic Odenwald backdrop later motivate him to develop CATAN? Maybe.
>
> Board games did not play a big role in his childhood until he was given the game *Romans vs. Carthaginians* at the age of 11. Soon the ancient armies had left the game board and fought fierce battles on the floor of the children's room. Klaus added new rules to the game and is now convinced that the foundation stone for his later game developments was laid during this time. After graduating from high school and doing military service, he studied

> chemistry. After completing his intermediate diploma, he joined his father's dental laboratory for family reasons. To compensate for the often very stressful everyday working life, Klaus began developing games in the early 1980s.
>
> ("*About the Catan GMBH*")

It's basically the plot of *Kinky Boots*, but with board games instead of thigh highs. And I don't know about you, but I can *feel* the eyebrow raise and satisfied look at the end of that first paragraph. Anyway, from there Teuber made a handful of games, four of which won the Spiel des Jahres ("Ludography"). Teuber's oeuvre is mostly concerned with feedback loop economics in grounded or historical settings and exploring worlds through their material circumstances. It's a bit more like a spreadsheet than I generally prefer, but I like stylization.

Speaking of stylization let's talk about Yoko Taro.

FIGURE 3.1 Yoko Taro in 2018. Photograph by Axem Titanium, used under Creative Commons BY 2.0.

You could say Taro (Figure 3.1) is something of an eccentric. While I can understand wanting to maintain a private life, I would probably do that with sunglasses and a nondescript haircut. Also, it is BOLD to think any game director is in danger of becoming too famous. But maybe, in his case, there's something to it. Taro's most famous work, *Nier: Automata*, has sold over 10 million copies worldwide, two of which are mine (Serin). Its predecessor, *Nier*, has sold about 500,000 copies (Khan) and was itself a spin-off of *Drakengard 3*, which sold around 151,000 units. My copy of *Drakengard 3* doesn't count, since it's second-hand. The point is, Yoko Taro was on to something years ago and we, the playing audience, finally caught up. It also helped that he developed *Automata* with Platinum Games, best known for *Bayonetta*. You know, the game series about a dominatrix witch who kills angels by channeling demons through portals made of her clothes. Taro and Platinum are well matched.

Taro, as far as I can find, does not have a biography predicated on "How he could not become an eccentric game director?" but there is an illuminating anecdote he shared in an interview promoting *Drakengard 3*. According to him, an acquaintance was walking along a shopping center roof and fell to his death. That's not the weird part. The weird part is that the dead man had an erection, so despite how shocking the situation was, everyone laughed. Taro used this story to explain his approach to writing characters with complex trauma responses (Kajita). Given that this story reads like a supervillain origin, making weird video games seems a very reasonable response on Taro's part.

What would be unreasonable would be to expect anyone to understand the timeline of Taro's oeuvre, but podcaster and journalist Chris Plante certainly has tried. He's something of an *Automata* evangelist, having spoken at length about the game on both his and others' podcasts, and writing about the series at Polygon.com. In the interest of keeping your interest, I'll take a cue from Plante and not worry too much about trying to make sense out of the timeline. It works better to treat it as a flower bed from which themes and ideas spring (Bigley). The first important thing is that the timeline of *Drakengard* and *Nier* is that it spans the three *Drakengard* games (Taro made the first and third) and the two *Nier* games along with manga, novels, radio dramas, concerts, and stage plays. Different aspects of the timeline branch off different games' endings, which are more or less simultaneous ("Timeline").

A by-no-means-complete list of events from this fictional history is as follows:

- The First Christmas
- Dragons burn down the Eastern Roman Empire
- A demigod attempts suicide which gives birth to her five sisters, One, Two, Three, Four, and Five. Of course her name is "Zero"
- "White Chlorination Syndrome," a degenerative disease caused by inhaling extradimensional magic, emerges in Shinjuku, Tokyo, Japan
- Scientists figure out how to divorce souls from bodies to buy time to cure White Chlorination Syndrome
- A magic homunculus creates a clone army of himself to wage a war against aliens

All this happens before *Nier: Automata* in much the same way that all of history up to now has preceded you reading this book. It's my contention that Yoko Taro basically wrote lore for *Drakengard* and then wrote a *library* of auto-fan fiction, a kind of *Silmarillion* for his world. Writing is fundamental in Taro's work. For instance, sentient books and a library of souls feature heavily in the first *Nier.* We'll focus on how his recurring thematic and formal ideas show up in *Automata.* Partly that's because it's the easiest of his games to get hold of in America, but also because it's the easiest to recommend as a fun game.

On that note: I would recommend playing *Automata* before reading further. I'd like for you to enjoy it yourself, whether or not you collect all the bracketed [e]ndings. Then again, if you're like me, an interesting enough spoiler might entice you to play a game you otherwise wouldn't. I want you to get the most you can out of the game and, hopefully, I can add to your enjoyment. Now, on with the show.

For someone who's written so damn *much* text, Taro's approach to authorship fits a man who'd wear a mask for public speaking. When asked how he felt seeing players talk about his games, he said, "I don't really like seeing discussions. That said, I also don't like it when people just accept my answers at face value... I once saw fan art depicting Devola and Popola

[*Nier* characters] as lesbians, and I thought to myself, 'Oh, that's how it was. I didn't know that'" (Kajita). When asked by the Japanese *PlayStation Magazine* questions about *Automata*, he ended every answer with some variation of, "I must be brief, so I'll leave out the details" ("Additional"). And unlike *some* authors who can't leave well enough alone on Twitter, Taro tweeted, "I'd like to share my thoughts on the characters from the 'YoRHa Boys' stage play and explore deeper into their feelings, but if the original creator does that, it [will] end up being considered official canon and limit everyone's imagination, so I can't say anything. Ugh!" ("Yokoverse FAQ")

It's a principled stance from an artist who wants his audience to let the author rest in peace, and that makes sense considering he bemoaned the lack of "weird" people making games (P Đorđe). Even so, he isn't above making a living (remember those earlier sales figures). When asked by *Game Informer* about fans pushing for Bandai Namco to add *Automata* protagonist 2B to *Tekken*'s roster of fighters, he said, "For us, if we were asked, we would gladly say yes to anything for money. We're open to any kind of opportunities for anything, ever. Even if it's *Candy Crush*, if they want to use 2B, we will say yes, please go ahead and use her" (Khan). And use her they have! 2B and other *Nier* characters have appeared in dozens of other games, ranging from fellow *Square Enix*-published *Final Fantasy XIV* to *Fall Guys*, which is about jellybean people falling down ("Crossovers"). This is on top of the *Automata* anime, novels, etc. Suffice to say, Taro is not precious about his work even as he dedicates himself to it.

A fan (or scholar) would have to be at least as dedicated to keep track of *Nier* canonicity. One of the hallmarks of Taro's work is his use of multiple endings. It's not new for a game to play around with endings and time: *Metal Gear Solid* and *Silent Hill 2* made great use of repeating play and alternate endings. In those cases, there is either a "correct" ending or endings that are just for laughs, like *Silent Hill 2*'s "dog in a spaceship." What makes Taro's endings more robust is that, by building alternate timelines into the story, anything in the text is "true" depending on the dimension. Even though *Automata*, at least in the English version, calls them "endings," it might be more useful to call them something like "routes" (Bigley). There can't be a correct ending to *Nier* because *Nier* doesn't end. It's just that sometimes players get further in the telling… in one direction or another.

Automata calls on the original *Nier* for some of its meaning, but many of the game's most interesting facets reach out to philosophy texts. Philosophizing may not be the most emotionally affecting, but you don't need me to tell you how haunting a robot circus is or how upsetting it is to watch robots go through the motions of an orgy. You need me (well, maybe not *need*) to tell you what makes Taro's work odder than it needs to be in ways you don't have to notice to enjoy his games. A lot of *Automata*'s intertextuality hinges on character names, which isn't subtle, but *Automata* is a game about android soldiers who wear blindfolds taking orders from androids who veil their mouths, so subtlety isn't the order of the day.

Taro, meaning to or not, includes himself in *Nier*'s tapestry. His signature mask is the head of Emil, a prominent character in *Nier* who appears in *Automata*. Taro named Emil after the Brothers Grimm's younger brother Ludwig Emil Grimm and received magic powers as part of the "Snow White Program" to combat White Chlorination Syndrome (Loe 74). In our reality, Emil is the face of *Nier*, and he is Yoko Taro. *Drakengard/Nier* lore partially takes place in our reality, so there's no reason not to read Taro's headgear as Emil literally living on our Earth. He's the one character who survives the approximately 8,475 years between *Nier* and *Automata*; why shouldn't he attend the Tokyo Game Show?

Taro, in his madness, was not content to implicate only himself and Ludwig Grimm. *Automata* is rife with allusions to texts and writers, including the player characters. Over the course of *Automata*, players control 2B, 9S, and A2. "2B" is an overt play on Hamlet's soliloquy, "To be or not to be," while "9S" is probably a pun from the Latin "non esse" or "not to be" ("Yorha No.9 Type S"). Rounding out the Shakespearean references, "A2" sounds an awful lot like Julius Cesar's dying words, "et tu, Brute?" "2B" feels ham-fisted in a game about sad robots, but it invites reflection and foreshadows the plot.

For convenience's sake, here is Hamlet's soliloquy:

> To be, or not to be, that is the question,
> Whether 'tis nobler in the mind to suffer
> The slings and arrows of outrageous fortune,
> Or to take arms against a sea of troubles,
> And by opposing end them? To die: to sleep;
> No more; and by a sleep to say we end

The heart-ache and the thousand natural shocks
That flesh is heir to, 'tis a consummation
Devoutly to be wish'd. To die, to sleep;
To sleep: perchance to dream: ay, there's the rub;
For in that sleep of death what dreams may come
When we have shuffled off this mortal coil,
Must give us pause: there's the respect
That makes calamity of so long life;
For who would bear the whips and scorns of time,
The oppressor's wrong, the proud man's contumely,
The pangs of despised love, the law's delay,
The insolence of office and the spurns
That patient merit of the unworthy takes,
When he himself might his quietus make
With a bare bodkin? who would fardels bear,
To grunt and sweat under a weary life,
But that the dread of something after death,
The undiscover'd country from whose bourn
No traveller returns, puzzles the will
And makes us rather bear those ills we have
Than fly to others that we know not of?
Thus conscience does make cowards of us all;
And thus the native hue of resolution
Is sicklied o'er with the pale cast of thought,
And enterprises of great pith and moment
With this regard their currents turn awry,
And lose the name of action.--Soft you now!
The fair Ophelia! Nymph, in thy orisons
Be all my sins remember'd.

Hamlet, the failed prince of Denmark, muses whether it would be better to shuffle off this mortal coil because everything is bad or not kill himself because death might be worse. This is, basically, the plot of *Automata*, a story bookended with suicide and mutually assured destruction. In the game's overture, 2B and 9S are injured and surrounded by enemies. They decide to blow themselves up, not knowing whether their memories will be resurrected in new bodies. *Automata*'s fullest and furthest [e]nding has 9S and A2 fight to their mutual deaths. Unlike Hamlet, our android heroes(?)

are willing to proclaim the name of action. In the [e]nd, A2 reveals to 9S that 2B wasn't a "B" unit. She was 2E, for "executioner," meaning she was 2E and not 2B.

A2's eponym is a bit more straightforward. *Julius Caesar*'s midpoint is the titular character getting assassinated by the Roman senate. He asks "Et tu, Brute?" as his best friend Brutus finally kills him (Caesar thoughtfully kept the Latin to a minimum for English-speaking audiences). Mission support initially tells players A2 is a rogue unit and orders 2B and 9S to kill her. Eventually, A2 mercy-kills 2B which leads 9S to fight her to their mutual deaths.

That is the last boss fight before the final [e]nding, in which the credits roll and the androids' support Pods begin to delete everything related to Project YoRHa. The two of them, and presumably the player, wish 2B, 9S, and A2 could have survived. The Pods decide they can restore all three of them. If the player agrees to help, the credits become a "bullet hell shooter," like a much harder *Asteroids*. It's punishing, but not only in how much the player dies: the game mocks and disparages the player when it asks whether to continue. That is, until it doesn't. The player receives messages of help and encouragement from other people who have beaten the game, the inverse of how the player found other players' corpses throughout their adventure.

Once the player has destroyed the credits and KILLED GOD/Yoko Taro, the game asks the player if they'd like to offer their own message of hope and support at the cost of deleting their own save data. The game goes so far as to warn the player that they might help someone they wouldn't even like if they met. When I was a kid and got to the end of a long game, I would play and rewatch the ending over and over again. I don't do that now, but I like having a save file around the way I like full bookshelves. Still, I agreed to help; it felt meaningful and good, and I've always been glad I did it. That is, until now, when I wanted to replay the ending to write about it. Even with the debug mode, I'd have to level up my characters to finish the last fight and that means playing through much of the game. It wasn't to be.

I mentioned *Automata*'s odd ending to my friend and LARP designer Carly Dwyer of Intramersive Media. Her response was, "It's like *The Tempest*." I talked to her about it a bit more, and the overlap is strong enough that I'm inclined to believe it's intentional. If it isn't, it's still a terrific insight. I've included her reading at the end of this chapter.

Taro wasn't content to name *Automata*'s population only with Shakespeare references and descriptors like "Small Stubby" and "Medium Flyer." A rose by any other name does not smell just as sweet, which is why the Machine Circus has Romeo and Juliet units. Of course, after the machines put on the play, they lose it and start killing each other. All the game's denizens face the end of their designed usefulness, and Taro tasks them to find a reason to live. The story stress-tests those reasons by naming robots after philosophers, and of them the lucky few are those the player kills.

Automata's first boss is a "Marx" unit, which is a giant bucket-wheel excavator. Later, two of Marx form the arms of an Engels unit. There's a dark comedy in naming robots after Karl Marx and Friedrich Engels, co-writers of *The Communist Manifesto*: if you can't seize the means of production, become them. More irreverent still, players will take control of these units to attack other machines. There's even a quest wherein players restore a debilitated Engels enough to speak. He asks for stories about the past, says he wants to see the stars, and tells the androids that machines have no concept of "sin."

Given time to reflect, Engels decides he did sin by killing legions of androids and inflicting "anguish" on the survivors. He elects to die as recompense, forcing 2B to realize androids are guilty of the same evil. It's a step toward class consciousness, which makes sense given that Engels and Marx's work framed history as the struggle between the ruling classes and the working classes. In *Automata*, the ruling class, the humans, are gone, and their creations are left to figure it out.

The idea that humans are not beholden to a design and are responsible for their own actions is a core tenet of existentialism as explored by de Beauvoir, Sartre, and Nietzsche. And wouldn't you know it? There are machines named after them, too. 2B and 9S fight Simone (as in "de Beauvoir") in a Machine Circus theater decorated with android corpses. Simone's body is similarly adorned, but the body itself is made of other machines. She's something like the combination of a prima donna and a tank. In her description, the game confirms she murdered other machines to construct herself (and to catch Jean-Paul's eye, no less).

It is a disturbing, literal, and disturbingly literal take on Beauvoir's argument that social conditions produce womanhood: "One is not born, but rather becomes, a woman" (Beauvoir 273). It seemed to me, at first, that characterizing Beauvoir as cannibalistic was tasteless. I had no problem with the crucified androids. That was self-defense! Probably! I just didn't appreciate the metaphor, intentional or not, that Beauvoir used other women to advance herself. Then I realized I don't know that much about *The Second Sex* and its author. After a little reading, I'm fine with the Simone boss fight.

In her critique of *The Second Sex*, Dr. Kathryn Belle argues that Beauvoir didn't consider racialized women in her feminism. "After all," Belle quotes Beauvoir on what should replace patriarchy, "the American slaves didn't ask themselves what was going to happen to the American economy when they won their freedom" (Belle 305). That sounds like something a boss enemy might say in the middle of a fight, though not in *Automata*: they wouldn't know what an "America" is.

They do know what a community is, though. *Automata*'s machines, emulating humans, established a village in the woods. This is where players meet Jean-Paul (as in "Sartre"). Curious players can talk to him and follow the "Jean-Paul's Melancholy" quest, because of course he's a sad robot. It's a "fetch quest" sending players thither and yon to collect tribute from Jean-Paul's female admirers. He is ambivalent toward the tokens and hostile to his admirers' desire for his attention ("Is one duty-bound to reply to every question spewed in their direction?"). His indifference is something of a mischaracterization of Sartre, though one could argue his disinterest stems from the adherents in question are adults and therefore too old for him. He and Beauvoir "developed a pattern, which they called the 'trio,' in which Beauvoir would seduce her students and then pass them on to Sartre." It's especially upsetting because the village was founded by another philosopher-bot specifically to protect children. And what a guardian they have in Pascal the pacifist.

Pascal starts as a typical quest-giving, resource-having NPC who teaches philosophy—he's skeptical of Nietzsche's declaration that "God is dead"— and emotions to other machines. His hatred of violence shocks 2B and 9S, but by now the player has encountered passive machines.

During an attack on the village, Pascal asks for A2's help; some of his villagers start "eating their fellow machines" ("Pascal"). The craze is part of a larger attack, so once A2 and Pascal get the children to safety, Pascal hijacks an Engels unit to defend them. Upon returning to the children to let them know it's safe, Pascal discovers they killed themselves to escape the fear he taught them to feel.

Pascal's namesake is the 17th-century philosopher Blaise Pascal, famous for "Pascal's Wager." The wager argues people should believe in the God of the Christian Bible because if he is real and a person believes, they go to heaven; if he is not real and someone believes, they lose nothing; if he is real and they don't believe, they burn in Hell forever and ever, amen (Pascal 67).

But if someone believes in god and he is not real, don't they stand to lose something? In *Automata*, Pascal abandons his philosophical position to save children. He's correct to do so, but it is that philosophical position that guided his actions up to that point, including imparting the concept of fear. His belief that pacifism would protect his village informed his actions until that belief failed. That same belief led to mass suicide.

Surrounded by death and apostasy, Pascal asks A2 to wipe his memory or kill him. The player can do either of those or just walk away. If A2 does delete his memory, he becomes a shopkeeper in the village. He sells parts of the dead children. He doesn't know enough for that to strike him as horrible (Bigley). All philosophies fail eventually, but relationships don't, and that is *Automata*'s [e]nding.

While I was writing this chapter, Square Enix announced, appropriately cryptically, that more *Nier* is coming. Whatever it is, I'm happy Taro is still cultivating his bizarre spin-off of his marginally successful action game about dragons. On the heels of that news, it was also announced that Taro will be writing the new *Neon Genesis Evangelion* series. For those unfamiliar, suffice to say *Evangelion* is the reason Millennials who watch anime are so traumatized (in a fun way).

If the contemporary, mainstream auteur is someone whose voice comes through in an established IP, Taro has managed to make that true even in his own series. *Drakengard* and *Nier* are so odd and so franchised that it feels as though he is relaying the history of another dimension. For a Westerner such as myself, it feels that way partly because *Automata* was a revelation, appearing to come out of nowhere fully formed like Android-thena from the head of Robo-Zeus. My only concern is that the new *Evangelion* will be too "Yoko Taro." If that's the case, I still want to see how.

In criticism, having a lot of material to explore is a good problem to have. Artists' ideas and approaches change, with different works qualifying, refuting, and building on one another. There's value for other artists in studying those changes: considering another artist's obsessions is a good way to realize and cultivate one's own. There is a more immediate and vital lesson, though. Taro is just one example, albeit an excellent one: artists often don't get jobs because they make art "correctly." There's plenty of pressure to "know the rules before you break them," but there are no rules, just questions. The first is, "Is this interesting?" and above all else, Yoko Taro's games are that.

This is the interview with fellow game designer Carly Dwyer on how *Automata*'s end mirrors *The Tempest*. Dwyer studied Shakespeare throughout her college education and has directed almost all of his plays, which is what led her to creating high-production value live-action role-playing games about social tension and monstrosity. You can find her work at intramersive.com.

I've edited for clarity.

B: Hi! Could you basically repeat what you just told me?

Carly: My understanding of *Nier Automauta*'s ending is the player cannot complete the game and release the characters without employing help from the community and sacrificing their save file. Combining that with game's other Shakespearean references makes me think this ending references Prospero's last speech in *The Tempest*.

B: My Shakespeare isn't good. Tell me a bit more about *The Tempest*?

Carly: It's understood to be Shakespeare's last play, written after giving up his role at the Globe Theater and moving back to Stratford to live out his retirement with his wife and adult daughters.

The Tempest is a play about a man reckoning with the power granted to him by creativity, the role he plays in a growing world, the harm he has caused, the legacy he leaves behind, and ultimately his own mortality. It is also one of the only times (maybe THE only time) a character recognizes the audience, and the fact they're in a play, in a non-comedic context.

B: How does Prospero come to terms with all that?

Carly: He's atoned for his sins, repaired his relationship with his brother, embraced his daughter's love for Ferdinand, freed Caliban and Ariel (the manifestation of creativity), and returns the island to its indigenous population. Even then, he's not freed from his mortal obligations.

B: My Shakespeare is not good. What does all that mean in the context of the story?

Carly: He has been the culture leader, he's designed the islanders' dreams, and he has held the world together in the image he created. He can undo his magic and make amends to the characters in his story, but he cannot be relieved of his duties without the audience's permission. Much like Shakespeare, who can put the pen down and walk away from the theatre, Prospero needs to know he's done enough to fulfill his purpose.

Before he can accept the humility of his old age and death, Prospero needs the audience to release him. Prospero kept everyone in the play under his control through magic, and he is likewise beholden to the audience. I see this mirrored in how YoRHa and the Machine Network internally drive *Automata*'s eternal war. It can only be resolved by the player, not the characters, sacrificing their own work to help others. If the player does not end the game by deleting their game data and walking away with only their memories, then the characters are trapped in forever war. It's much like how Shakespeare writes:

> Now I want
> Spirits to enforce, art to enchant,
> And my ending is despair,
> Unless I be relieved by prayer (Audiences bringing their hands together in applause),
> Which pierces so that it assaults
> Mercy itself, and frees all faults.
>
> (*The Tempest* Act V)

B: Could you talk a bit about what this means?

Carly: The end goal of *Automata* is for the characters to find peace in their existence outside of the war, outside of their duty to humanity, and outside the role of the player's entertainer. Likewise, the player is meant to finish the game and release themselves and the characters from the experience. They completed the art, they carry it with them, and everyone can move beyond this moment.

The full final monologue:

> Now my charms are all o'erthrown,
> And what strength I have 's mine own,
> Which is most faint. Now 'tis true
> I must be here confined by you,
> Or sent to Naples. Let me not,
> Since I have my dukedom got
> And pardoned the deceiver, dwell
> In this bare island by your spell,
> But release me from my bands
> With the help of your good hands.
> Gentle breath of yours my sails
> Must fill, or else my project fails,
> Which was to please. Now I want
> Spirits to enforce, art to enchant,
> And my ending is despair,
> Unless I be relieved by prayer,
> Which pierces so that it assaults
> Mercy itself, and frees all faults.
> As you from crimes would pardoned be,
> Let your indulgence set me free (Act V)

BIBLIOGRAPHY

"1999 State of the Industry." *Entertainment Software Association*, www.theesa.com/wp-content/uploads/2024/02/1999-IDSA-SOTI.pdf. Accessed 8 Feb. 2026.

"2013年度ゲームソフト販売ランキングTOP100!　1位は2バージョン合計で411万本を販売した3DS『ポケットモンスター X·Y』が獲得." 電撃オンライン, Japan dengekionline.com/elem/000/000/848/848437/. Accessed 22 Feb. 2026.

"About the Catan GMBH." CATAN, www.catan.com/explore-catan/ludography. Accessed 16 Feb. 2026.

Alexiel, Rekka, translator. "Additional Questions for Yoko Taro by Dengeki PlayStation." Fire Sanctuary, 19 Feb. 2019, https://firesanctuary.com/2019/02/19/additional-questions-for-yoko-taro-by-dengeki-playstation/.

Alexiel, Rekka. "Yokoverse FAQ." Fire Sanctuary. https://docs.google.com/spreadsheets/d/1DtXBGvR7rAxlApjf3n3uR3oH2keZ6c4RQvzUaJ2jj0U/edit?gid=1702175405gid=1702175405.

"Annual ESA Study Reveals Video Games' Universal Appeal across Generations." *Entertainment Software Association*, 4 June 2025, www.theesa.com/annual-esa-study-reveals-video-games-universal-appeal-across-generations/:~:text=Players%20represent%20every%20demographic.,and%20are%20educational%20(70%25).

"Antoine Bauza." Board Game Geek, 16 Feb. 2026, https://boardgamegeek.com/boardgamedesigner/9714/antoine-bauza.\

"Automata Units." NieR Wiki, Fandom, Inc. https://nier.fandom.com/wiki/Category:NieR:Automata_Units. Accessed 6 March 2026.

Bahr, Fax and Hickenlooper, George. *Hearts of Darkness: A Filmmaker's Apocalypse*. Triton Pictures, United States, 1991.

"Batman." *Box Office Mojo*, www.boxofficemojo.com/release/rl3695543809/. Accessed 3 Feb. 2026.

"Batman Returns." *Box Office Mojo*, https://www.boxofficemojo.com/title/tt0103776/. Accessed 3 Feb. 2026.

Baker, Vincent. "Powered by the Apocalypse, Part 1." Lumpley Games, lumpley.games/2019/12/30/powered-by-the-apocalypse-part-1/. Accessed 17 Feb. 2026.

Baker, D. Vincent, and Meguey Baker. *Dogs in the Vineyard*. Lumpley Games, United States, 2004.

Bauza, Antoine. *Ghost Stories*. Repos Production, United States, 2008.

Bauza, Antoine. Hanabi. R&R Games, United States, 2010.

Bauza, Antoine, and Naiade. *Tokaido*. Fun Forge, United States, 2014.

Belle, Kathryn Sophia. *Beauvoir and Belle: A Black Feminist Critique of the Second Sex*. Oxford University Press, Oxford, United Kingdom, 2024.

Bigley, Brendon and Hilger, Stephen. "Spelunky + Nier: Automata (w/Guest Chris Plante)." *Into the Aether*. Podcast. Season 3 bonus episode, Aug. 2020.

Bordwell, David. *On the History of Film Style*. Irvington Way Press, United States, 2028.

Boss, Emily Care. *Under My Skin*. Black & Green Games, United States, 2010.

Burton, Tim and Jack Nicholson. *Batman*. Warner Bros., United States, 1989.

Burton, Tim and Michael Keaton. *Batman Returns*. Warner Bros., United States, 1992.

"Crossovers." *NieR Wiki*, Fandom, Inc., nier.fandom.com/wiki/Crossovers. Accessed 26 Feb. 2026.

De Beauvoir, Simone. *The Second Sex*. Translated by H.M. Parshley, Lowe and Brydone, New York, United States, 1953.

Elderkin, Beth. "GDC 2026 State of the Game Industry Reveals Impact of Layoffs, Generative AI, and More." Game Developers Conference, Jan. 2026, gdconf.com/article/gdc-2026-state-of-the-game-industry-reveals-impact-of-layoffs-generative-ai-and-more/:~:text=Majority%20of%20Game%20Workers%20Would,interested%20in%20joining%20a%20union.

Ganz, Megan. "Documentary Filmmaking: Redux." Community, season 3, episode 8, 17 Nov. 2011.

Green, Lorien. "Going Cardboard: A Board Game Documentary." *YouTube*, www.youtube.com/watch?v=JmZ1J6V_8Sg. Accessed 15 Feb. 2026.

Groen, Andrew. "The Death March: The Problem of Crunch Time in Game Development." Ars Technica, 27 May 2011, arstechnica.com/gaming/2011/05/the-death-march-the-problem-of-crunch-time-in-game-development/.

Đorđe, P. "Nier: Automata Creator Yoko Taro Says There Are Less 'Weird' People in the Gaming Industry Nowadays." AUTOMATON WEST, 18 June 2025, automaton-media.com/en/news/nier-automata-creator-yoko-taro-says-there-are-less-weird-people-in-the-gaming-industry-nowadays/.

"Heritage of the Past." NieR Wiki, Fandom, Inc., nier.fandom.com/wiki/Heritage_of_the_Past. Accessed 2 March 2026.

"Hideo Kojima: Connecting Worlds (2023)." IMDb, www.imdb.com/title/tt26739107/. Accessed 18 Feb. 2026.

Hitchcock, Alfred. *Rear Window*. Paramount Pictures, United States, 1954.

Huizinga, Johan. *Homo Ludens: A Study of the Play-Element in Culture*. Routledge & K. Paul, London, United Kingdom, 1949.

Kajita, Mafia. "Thoughts on the Game Industry Surrounded by an 'Invisible Wall.'" *4Gamer.Net*, 1 March 2014, www.4gamer.net/games/207/G020792/20140221105/.

Khan, Imran. "Talking to Yoko Taro, PlatinumGames' Takahisa Taura, and Composer Keiichi Okabe about Life, Death, and Opportunity." *Game Informer*, 1 Jan. 2019, gameinformer.com/2019/01/01/talking-to-yoko-taro-platinumgames-takahisa-taura-and-composer-keiichi-okabe-about-life.

Klimek, Chris. "Analysis | the Sequels That Snatched Defeat from the Victory of 'Jaws.'" *The Washington Post*, 14 June 2025, www.washingtonpost.com/entertainment/movies/2025/06/14/jaws-sequels/.

Kojima, Hideo. *Death Stranding*. PlayStation 5. Kojima Productions, 2019.

Kojima, Hideo. *Metal Gear Solid*. PlayStation. Konami, 1998.

Kojima, Hideo. *Metal Gear Solid 2: Sons of Liberty*. PlayStation 2. Konami, 2001.

"Ko-Shi & Ro-Shi." NieR Wiki, Fandom, Inc. https://nier.fandom.com/wiki/https://nier.fandom.com/wiki/Ko-Shi_%26_Ro-Shi. Accessed 6 March 2026.

Korman, Jonathan. "Dogs In The Vineyard." Itch.io, 2025, https://miniver.itch.io/ditv:~:text=Designer%20Vincent%20Baker%20has%20taken,moral%20implications%20of%20the%20setting.

Loe, Casey, et al. *Grimoire Nier, Revised Edition: Project Gestalt & Replicant System: Nier Replicant Ver. 1.22474487139: The Complete Guide*. Square Enix Manga & Books, Tokyo, Japan, 2023.

"Ludography." *CATAN*, www.catan.com/explore-catan/ludography. Accessed 15 Feb. 2026.

Lynch, David and Kyle MacLachlan. *Dune*. Universal Pictures, United States, 1984.

Martin, Andy. "Savile, Beauvoir and the Lolita Syndrome - The New York Times." *New York Times Archive*, 19 May 2013, archive.nytimes.com/opinionator.blogs.nytimes.com/2013/05/19/savile-beauvoir-and-the-charms-of-the-nymph/.

Miller, Glen. *Hideo Kojima: Connecting Worlds*. Filmworks London, United Kingdom, 2023.

Morris, Allison Michelle. A History of the Summer Blockbuster, 13 July 2024, www.allisonmichellemorris.com/post/history-summer-blockbusters.

Parkin, Jeffrey. "Nier Replicant Guide: Every Weapon and Where to Find Them." *Polygon*, 22 April 2021, www.polygon.com/nier-replicant-guide-walkthrough-ver-1-22474487139/22393850/weapon-every-all-location-one-two-handed-lance-spear/lTdiH8.

Pascal, Blaise. "Pascal's Pensées." E.P. Dutton & Co., Boston, United States, 1958.

"Pascal." NieR Wiki, Fandom, Inc., nier.fandom.com/wiki/Pascal. Accessed 2 March 2026.

Serin, Kaan, and George Young. "Nier Automata 'to Be Continued,' Square Enix Says, Giving Stunned Fans Some Hope as the Yoko Taro-Led JRPG Flies Past 10 Million Copies Sold." *GamesRadar+*, GamesRadar+, 20 Feb. 2026, www.gamesradar.com/games/jrpg/nier-automata-to-be-continued-square-enix-says-giving-stunned-fans-some-hope-as-the-yoko-taro-led-jrpg-flies-past-10-million-copies-sold/.

Shakespeare, William. Hamlet. United Kingdom, https://shakespeare.mit.edu/hamlet/full.html.

Shakespeare, William. Julius Caesar. United Kingdom, https://www.gutenberg.org/files/1522/1522-h/1522-h.htm.

Shakespeare, William. The Tempest. United Kingdom, https://shakespeare.mit.edu/tempest/full.html.

"Spear of the Usurper (Nier)." NieR Wiki, Fandom, Inc., nier.fandom.com/wiki/Spear_of_the_Usurper_(Nier). Accessed 2 March 2026.

Stanton, Rich. "A Brief History of Metal Gear Solid." IGN, 30 Aug. 2016, United Kingdom, www.ign.com/articles/2015/07/29/a-brief-history-of-metal-gear-solid.

Taro, Yoko. *Nier: Automata*. PlayStation 4. Square Enix, 2017.

Taro, Yoko. *Nier Replicant ver.1.22474487139...* PlayStation 4. Square Enix, 2021.

Teuber, Klaus. *The Settlers of Catan*. Franchk-Kosmos Verlag, 1995.

Thompson, Kristin. "A24: The Studio as Auteur." *Observations on Film Art*, 10 Oct. 2022, www.davidbordwell.net/blog/2022/10/10/a24-the-studio-as-auteur/.

"Timeline." Nier Wiki, Fandom, Inc., https://nier.fandom.com/wiki/Timeline. Accessed 23 Feb. 2026.

Tsukamoto, Shinya. *Tetsuo*: The Iron Man." Kaijyu Theatre, Japan, 1989.

"Virtuous Contract (Nier)." NieR Wiki, Fandom, Inc., nier.fandom.com/wiki/Virtuous_Contract_(NieR). Accessed 2 March 2026.

Webb, Hope. "Grand Theft Auto: Game Creator Sacked Us for Trying to Unionise." *BBC News*, BBC, 15 Dec. 2025, www.bbc.com/news/articles/cp89990rgdno.

"YoRHa-issue Blade." *NieR Wiki*, Fandom, Inc., nier.fandom.com/wiki/YoRHa-issue_Blade. Accessed 2 Marc 2026.

"Yorha No.9 Type S." *NieR Wiki*, Fandom, Inc., nier.fandom.com/wiki/YoRHa_No.9_Type_S. Accessed 4 March 2026.

CHAPTER 4

Long Playing

Games as Music

I have this theory, maybe more of a thought, that a lot of games are "karaoke for X." Playing an NBA game is not like playing basketball, but it is a chance to play at being good at basketball. It drove my parents nuts that I would spend an entire weekend playing *Harvest Moon 64* but whine about taking care of our chickens. They didn't understand that I wasn't playing the game because I wanted to raise chickens. *Harvest Moon 64* (and the much-more-recent *Stardew Valley*) is not really about farming as much as it's about being part of a farming community. Also, video game chickens have the advantage of not generating feces.

Music games, especially *Rock Band* and *Guitar Hero*, suffered more from adults' misunderstanding. "Why not just play the guitar?" went the rhetorical question. But *Rock Band* wasn't about playing the guitar or singing, although its drum kit was basically a real electronic drum set. *Rock Band* was karaoke for being a rock star. Actually learning to play the guitar is hard and tedious. I tried. I quickly realized I didn't actually want to play the guitar. What I wanted was to enjoy music with friends, and a video game was much better for that than doing something I didn't want to do for its own sake.

What I wanted to do was play games. I'm glad I stayed up so many nights playing *Rock Band* with my friends because one of the great things about music is how it surfaces feelings and memories. Like a film soundtrack, a

DOI: 10.1201/9781003755821-4

video game's music evokes how a scene or sequence made us feel or what it was like at the time in our life when we first heard that song. The difference between game and movie soundtracks is that when someone wants to experience a particular scene in a movie, they can just fast forward to the scene. Video games are, in this sense, more linear than films, but a game's soundtrack can get a player into that memory without trudging through a tutorial level or a tedious quest. On top of being art in their own right, video game soundtracks are convenient.

Some soundtracks are about their games, some games are about their soundtracks. *Rock n' Racing*, for instance, was a Super Nintendo racing game that actually looks pretty fun, but probably wouldn't be remembered if not for its soundtrack, which includes weirdly good MIDI versions of "Bad To The Bone" by George Thorogood, "Paranoid" by Black Sabbath, and "Highway Star" by Deep Purple. Blizzard, apparently, got the licenses for not a lot of money, which I guess means the rights holders didn't know how much this video game thing was going to catch on ("BlizzConline").

Other games and soundtracks are about one another in that they were made, or at least curated, for each other. The *Tony Hawk's Pro Skater* series exposed kids like me to punk, ska-punk, pop-punk, hardcore punk, and post-punk we might never have heard otherwise. It was a mixtape Hawk made for the players, and I still find myself humming tracks from it. Recently, *Tony Hawk's Pro Skater 1+2* remakes came out, bringing in new fans and platforming new bands (Regan).

Other games, like *D&D*, lend themselves very nicely to players making their own playlists: I fondly remember playing in the basement of a game store with *everyone* singing along to Evanescence's "My Immortal." It was the perfect tableau for my level 15 Storm Lord shooting rainbows at demons. Since so many tabletop games are attached to an existing franchise, their sound is pretty obvious. For example, *The One Ring: Roleplaying in the World of The Lord of the Rings* pairs nicely with Howard Shore's *The Lord of the Rings* soundtrack. *Cowboy Bebop*, the sci-fi Western/jazz anime, has a tabletop game, as do *Blade Runner* and *Alien*. Some tabletop authors like to list their inspirations so players can get into the game's groove. I did something similar with my game *Very Pleasant Queer Makeover Show* thinking that, as long as someone was reading the rulebook, I might as well go all-in on being a nerd.

I'm interested in understanding games as albums themselves and viewing them through the lens of music genre, even if the game doesn't provide any music. Two of my favorites are *Misspent Youth* and *Sayonara Wild Hearts*. A "gamey" way to describe *Misspent Youth* would be "a story-forward roleplaying game." But really, it's a punk rock game. *Sayonara Wild Hearts* is a lyrical video game, both in the sense that it's poetic in its meaning and structure and that it's got songs with words. It's a hyperpop or vaporwave album you play. These titles aren't games with soundtracks as much as they are albums with playtracks.

"Punk" as a suffix gets thrown around a lot these days. "Cyberpunk" is top-of-mind thanks to *Cyberpunk 2077*, the CD Projekt Red game based on the tabletop RPG, but there is a handful of other "-punks" because there's no genre you can't over-atomize. There's steampunk and diesel-punk, which are at least partly based on aesthetic elements: Victorian era-ish science fiction and the something along the lines of *Mad Max*, respectively.

Then there are less specific "-punks." There's "hopepunk," which means the story is optimistic as an answer to "grimdark" storytelling (Romano). As a genre, the term doesn't accomplish anything that one can't do by saying a story is "hopeful." Part of what makes something a genre in any useful sense is that it points toward some aesthetic, and maybe contextual, elements so everyone in the conversation can know they're talking about more or less the same thing.

The flipside is people in games using genre descriptors too specifically or perfectly vaguely. Calling *Metroid or Castlevania* a "metroidvania" is like describing *The Metamorphosis* as "Kafkaesque" a la *The Squid and the Whale* (Baumbach). For vagary, "roguelite" has been applied widely enough that it means next to nothing.

As cyberpunk is so popular in games and broadly accepted as an artistic subgenre, it would be good to contextualize it a bit before digging more deeply into punk and *Misspent Youth*. Like most genres, most ideas, it's more useful to describe it than to define it. The writer Bruce Sterling taglined cyberpunk as "high tech, low life," which feels about perfect to me (Norbez). The genre, it is generally understood, was started by Bruce Bethke's 1983 short story "Cyberpunk" (Norbez) and popularized by William Gibson's novel *Neuromancer*.

Movies helped establish the cyberpunk "look," even if they predated the term. 1982's *Blade Runner* and 1989's *Akira*—based on the 1982 manga—are both early, high-profile examples people point to with deserved regularity. Both movies visualize what Bethke and Gibson suggested: decrepit urban hellscapes pulsing in neon and navigated with very cool cars and computers. Shame about the corporate overlords, though.

People in the 80s were, understandably, concerned about corporations taking over America. Ronald Reagan, an actor who convinced people that giving the rich more money would get working people more money, was elected US president in '81. That's when *Dungeons & Dragons* had its initial surge of popularity, and it's a weirdly poetic coincidence that the game was largely oriented toward hoarding gold and hiring minions. Seven years later, game designer Mike Pondsmith was tired of high fantasy and wanted a sci-fi alternative, so he wrote and published *Cyberpunk* ("Cyberpunk Reflections"). Cyberpunk, like punk before it, started and persists as a response to mainstream style, whether that style is swords and sorcery or buttoned-up respectability.

To kick things off with criticism, one problem I have with *Cyberpunk 2077* is that players can take missions from cops, which is decidedly not punk. Sure, "punk rock is old enough to [be] your parents' music" (Rollins xiv), but punk is necessarily anti-establishment. It's not just a sound (buzzsaws at work on their willing victims) or a look (black leather and spikes) that makes something punk. It's an ethos. Thinking punk can be conservative ignores its history. From Marlaria! breaking into East Berlin shops to use them as venues, to Pussy Riot struggling against the Putin regime, punk and its performers are necessarily radically left (Goldman 190). It's worth mentioning because, despite being a forty-five-year-old song, the scene still needs Dead Kennedys' "Nazi Punks Fuck Off": "Punk means thinkin' for yourself/You ain't hardcore cuz you spike your hair/When a jock still lives inside your head/Nazi punks, fuck off."

That spirit is alive and well in *Misspent Youth*. I'll let the game introduce itself:

> Welcome to **Misspent Youth**. This is a fucking awesome game. You're gonna have fun with it. So much fun you'll wonder why it's not illegal. **Misspent Youth** is a science fiction game about friendship and rebellion. It's a roleplaying game, which means you create a world, pretend to be people you're not, and create a story in real time as you play the game. The protagonist in the stories you make is called a **Youthful Offender (YO)**, and is a heroic kid between 12 and 17 years old who won't put up with being oppressed. The antagonist is called **The Authority**, the force that's fucking up

> your world and making it a shitty place to live. You or one of your friends plays The Authority and everyone else plays a single YO.
>
> (i)

They wouldn't be allowed to print "you're gonna have fun" it if it weren't true, and I have had fun with it. After the introduction and listing some necessary materials and inspirations/recommendations, the game has players hit the ground running by creating The Authority (TA). What I find interesting about The Authority's design is how specific Bohl asks players to get. While "not every oppressor controls an entire planet" (Bohl 1), I would default to thinking that The Authority is a system and controls systems, so its motivations and hates would be as plentiful as there are bureaucrats. That's not great for storytelling, though, so *Misspent* asks players to pick from a list why TA does what it does and what its anathema is. It's an economical approach, since picking the concept TA hates (freedom, history, humanity, nature, or progress), the players choose what they defend. That simplification allows the party ("clique" in *Misspent*) to work together with a clear orientation.

Character creation starts with the usual kind of thing: name, age, some defining physical characteristics. Bohl encourages diverse characters and finds simply asking players about their gender and ethnicity is often enough to get people thinking past their defaults. Or, as he puts it, making a clique that's a "pasty sausage party" (Bohl 15). Whatever a "sausage party" is. "For me, having an entire rebel movement look like a '50s country club kinda gets in the way of expressing themes of revolt and rebellion" (Bohl 15). I am inclined to agree, though I will add that playing across ethnicities is something that should be done with care and consideration. If possible, it's probably better to diversify the gaming table. And if the table is at a country club, so somewhere else.

Misspent accounts for gender, but only two. The first time I played, the person playing The Authority told me pretty much what the rules say: the Personal Record/character sheet represents "The Authority's dossier on you. Fill in the circle that you think it would assign you as and use your Looks to express yourself on the character's gender identity." Any genderqueer character made according to the *Misspent* core book has to deal with some amount of misgendering. I'm not saying this is unrealistic.

Authoritarians tend to force people to check one box from a list of as few options as possible. But it's also true that players of any gender might not want to deal with transphobia. Maybe people want to imagine a world that isn't so OBSESSED with children's genitalia that the visible spectrum of light itself must correlate to gender roles. A girl can dream.

Misspents's first supplement, *Sell Out with Me,* maintains binary gender, except for an android who "presents as a boy" (Bohl 34). The second supplemental book, *FALL IN LOVE not in line*, opens up gender and species to all manner of fantasy races. This positions gender expression as necessarily related to romance, despite the fact of asexual trans people, and introduces trans folks along with elves does the disservice of presenting us as something other than "a regular human." In fairness, once you invite genderqueer folks, someone is going to want to play as an owlbear.

What I like best about *Misspent*'s core rules is how they structure story in play. The game provides players an overall story structure broken down by scenes. People who have only played *D&D* are sometimes used to running modules, or pre-built adventures tend to take care of pacing. Some other popular RPGs have modules as well, but indie games often have to do something to help players through scenes specifically, and stories in general. Laying out specific scenes and how they function narratively and mechanically helps players avoid the awkwardness of not knowing how or when to end a scene. The way "struggles" work in *Misspent* is very specifically structured and starts with a suitably punk sensibility: "The Authority asks, 'Who's gonna stand up?'" (Bohl 74) If TA is especially strait-laced, I imagine they will enunciate "going to." Then the conflict begins.

Players have a chart of the sums of two six-sided dice, one space for each number. The YO and TA take turns claiming spaces; YO's roll for theirs and The Authority takes them in a pattern set by the game rules for that scene. As the game goes on and the narrative stakes rise, The Authority takes more common rolls, like 7, sooner in the conflict (Aren't stats neat?). When a YO claims a space, they pick one of their convictions to use as their action (e.g., a character who's **fast** can run away from a guard and one who's **altruistic** could make friends and allies). If the YO lands on a space already claimed by the clique, the clique wins, cue power chords and "Oi"s. If the YO rolls an Authority space, the clique loses. That is, unless the idiot kid who screwed it up sells out.

If the YO sells out, the clique wins at a cost. For instance, someone who sold out their **tough** conviction would become **vicious**. The **outrage[d]** become **wrathful**, the **smart** become **pedantic**. As the campaign goes on, someone is going to sell out entirely. When that happens, the "series" is over and players tabulate how many convictions they kept versus how many they sold out to figure out their endings. The sellout definitely gets a bad ending, unless someone sacrifices their happy ending to the sellout. It's a teachable moment, and the sellout doesn't have a choice in the matter.

Playing *Misspent Youth* is karaoke-ing as a punk. The rulebook helps, since it's made to look like a zine and liner notes. Looking at it transports me back to when I was in high school and marveled at the poster that came with my copy of Dropkick Murphys' *Sing Loud, Sing Proud*. The rulebook design takes the lo-fi, DIY style that people had to use to reproduce flyers and magazines cheaply and makes it a deliberate choice. It's cool, sure, but more importantly it says that not while the rules have to be legible, they don't have to look *nice*.

The rules promise the opposite of a Hollywood ending. They promise No Future. The world will change, maybe even for the better. Playing the game feels like what I remember being a teenager felt like. I imagine a lot of teenagers have the sense of vast potential frustrated by adults' apathy and carelessness. Teenagers are nothing if not dramatic, and by symbolically killing a Youthful Offender at the end, the game invokes the Freudian death drive and puts the player in the kind of operatic drama only a teenager could take seriously. As Alan Moore put it in his introduction to Frank Miller's *The Dark Knight Returns*, "All of our best and oldest legends recognize that time passes and that people grow old and die. The legend of Robin Hood would not be complete without the final blind arrow shot to determine the site of his grave." *Misspent Youth* blends the fantasy of living fast and dying young with the necessity of myth.

That's not to say the game doesn't have a sense of humor. Each of the three books reminds the reader that fun is mandatory, and because I follow the rules, I'll offer up an account of the last time my friends and I played. Despite the anti-capitalism stance I share with *Misspent Youth*, I love a good shopping mall at Christmastime. It's cheery and colorful, and I like Christmas music, so obviously I wanted to stick that idea in the guts and twist the knife. Naturally, our Authority had to be an army of mall Santas: knows if you've been bad or good, he sees you when you're sleeping, etc. It's the logical conclusion to the surveillance state promised by Elf on a Shelf.

Yes, rumbling with a squadron of mall cops and robo-Santas is funny and fun, but the idea comes from real anxieties. Playing stories about police confiscating immigration lawyers' phones, checking people's social media for anti-American sentiment, or using AI-powered surveillance is much less fun. The people who hold power are so self-unaware that the easiest way to mock them is just saying out loud what they do, like naming a data and surveillance company after *The Lord of the Rings*' corrupted seeing stones. Dressing the panopticon like a jolly old elf and hitting it with a skateboard doesn't do anything materially, but I feel better after doing it and that ain't nothin'. Punk, at least in *Misspent*, isn't about how everything sucks and there can be no future. It's about how everything sucks, and we can do something right now.

I think part of why teenagers make music such a large part of their personalities is that music is so, so good at expressing big emotions. Lyrics can get at profound ideas, but they generally aren't (and probably shouldn't be) well-reasoned arguments. Stage musicals aren't about waxing philosophical; they're about cats who want to die and get reincarnated (or something). Music speaks to youthfulness because it's big enough to hold emotions you aren't sure what to do with, especially the feelings of getting dumped.

If I had to use digital store keywords to describe *Sayonara Wild Hearts*, I guess I'd call it a "musical racing game." *Sayonara* opens like a fairy tale. "Not long ago, in a town much like yours…" Queen Latifah says as gently as you'd read a bedtime story, there was a girl whose heart broke "so violently" it "echoed through space and time." The player character, The Fool, steps out of a falafel shop and skateboards out of frame. Cue main theme.

The color palette and language start the game with its definitive style. *Sayonara*'s waking world is a sleepy, unsaturated blue; the girl and her skateboard glow. The narration assures us of the story's timelessness, its ubiquity and simultaneity, which makes it sound like science fiction. It's sci-fi the way *Sailor Moon* is, in that it's a story about magic and emotions dancing to the music of the spheres. *Sayonara* isn't astronomical, though. It's astrological. The game's core motif is tarot, with characters aligned to the major arcana. This is less the case in video games (save the *Persona* series) than it is in tabletop tarot, which has become one of those concepts games need to give a rest. *Sayonara* gets away with it because its visual style guards the game against the pretension of spoooooky tarot art styles.

Players navigate a dream populated with Jungian archetypes, but I wouldn't call it surrealist. Maybe my dreams are boring and poorly lit, but *Sayonara* doesn't remind me of my dreams. Nor does it remind me of Maya Deren's or David Lynch's films. It's not that *Sayonara Wild Hearts* doesn't share aesthetics with, say, Frida Kahlo's work. The feeling comes more from the game functioning as a fairy tale. It's a psychodrama pop opera instead of an exploration of how our sleeping minds speak to us. It's a dream, yes, but it's not dreamy.

Sayonara's team describes it as, "at heart, a simple arcade game, controlled with a directional input and a button" ("Sayonara"). It's funny that "arcade" is the genre defined by that kind of play, often in the vein of being easy to learn and hard to master. My favorite arcade games are Capcom fighting games or something with a big, weird controller. Some arcade games are "rhythm games," which *Sayonara* is not, but "it follows the ebbs and flows of each track" ("Sayonara"). When the music swells, and The Fool hits a line of pickups which guide her through a neon canyon, it feels perfect.

More character-driven games thrive on little cinematics (e.g., karate guys charging energy blasts), and games with more plot usually have longer cutscenes. Here, the game taking control is the equivalent of breath marks for beleaguered woodwinds. The player still plays: "You can't exactly set the controller down and watch *Sayonara Wild Hearts* complete itself, as there are a number of sequences that require an active level of precision, but it's also a game that rarely burdens the player with much difficulty" (Klepek). That's the correct design choice. In fact, the weakest parts of *Sayonara Wild Hearts* are the parts that feel most like a video game.

When I say *Sayonara Wild Hearts* is an album and that's great, I mean it. It would be so much less interesting as a kind of music simulator with players approximating instruments. *Trombone Champ* exists, so video games as a medium have summited the mountain of games about playing music. That's why I wouldn't want *Sayonara* to be harder: it's a game of listening. It's also a game with high scores, a precious metals-based evaluation system, and unlockable levels. The secret levels are a brilliant addition—I was thrilled the first time I had an album with a secret track—but I can't help but wonder if it could shamelessly be a video game without having The Fool collect heart nubbins the way Sonic the Hedgehog collects rings.

Sayonara is great because it advances something else video games can be, and it does so by focusing on "video" at least as much as "game." By way of comparison, I have a deep affection for *Life is Strange*. *LiS* follows Max Caulfield, a high school girl with the ability to rewind time, as she investigates another young woman's disappearance. The gameplay and teenager slang have aged, but it's a tremendous story. The game cleverly opens with Max in her private high school's photography class as her teacher pontificates on Alfred Hitchcock, setting up the game's themes before Max explores her *Twin Peaks*-esque city. As she investigates the disappearance and reconnects with her problem-child best friend Chloe, Max scrubs through time to get around people's defenses, solve problems, and find evidence.

Max also gets a gun and shoots some bottles at a junkyard. Shooting stuff is what you do in video games.

It's not that shooting is necessarily more video gamey than investigating a probable murder, but it feels like a sequence inserted because that's what people expect from video games. Similar to *Sayonara*'s point collecting, the least interesting part of the game is when the design is an assumption of what games have to do. I hope future album video games build on *Sayonara Wild Hearts* and find different ways for players to listen by playing. All that said, it's a beautiful experience to dance as an arcade character, hurtling through black holes and electric pink valleys. Time changes shape, the skateboard's wheels roll at 33⅓ rpm, and as soon as The Fool goes back to bed, the player wants to begin again.

A lot of my training as an artist was developing how I think about and relate to time. There's the surface-level question of whether something is too long or too short, which amounts to whether something is boring or rushed. Pacing is an emotional, audience-facing phenomenon. On the process side of things, artists have to draw from different experiences of time and translate that for their audience. I love Tomonari Nishikawa's film *Market Street*, a five-minute film that uses the titular San Francisco street's shapes and shadows to animate abstraction. Even though I enjoy it, I'll admit it is a long five minutes.

Market Street is, like a lot of avant-garde films, "silent." The 16mm film doesn't have a soundtrack (in the sense that sound is not recorded on the film at all), and no online video I've seen has music or anything layered over it. Despite that, I hear the movie when I watch it. It's not that it suggests car horns or trolley bells. What I hear, and maybe this is because I was lucky enough to see Nishikawa present it in person, is a film projector whirring. *Market Street*'s beats make their own psychoacoustics, and they are the sounds a movie makes.

Which gets me wondering what future album games could be, how they could use the materials of games (controllers, keyboards, dice) to find new ways of playing and playful ways to listen.

In 2017, "hateful optimists and loving pessimists" Jocelyn Geddie and Kat Angus started *I Hate It But I Love It*, "a show about all the pop culture you love and hate simultaneously" ("About"). Since then, they have won a slew of awards, including Best Comedy Podcast (2019) and Best Television and Film Podcast (2025).

I've been listening for years and noticed that, while Kat and Jocelyn mention video games in relation to movies and TV, they don't get to talk about them at length. Jocelyn was kind enough to answer a few questions over email for me.

Out of respect for my neighbors to the North, I have left the "u" in "favourite." There are, however, slight edits for clarity.

B: What are some of your favorite games? What draws you to one game or another?

Jocelyn: Growing up, I played a lot of point-and-click PC adventure games. (For a long time, I nurtured a dream of working for Sierra Entertainment when I grew up!) So many of my favorite games fall under that umbrella: *LOOM*, *King's Quest 5: Absence Makes the Heart Go Yonder*, *King's Quest 6: Heir Today, Gone Tomorrow*, *King's Quest 7: The Princeless Bride*, and *Space Quest 6: The Spinal Frontier*. In recent years, my favourite games have included *Batman: Arkham City*, *Legend of Zelda: Tears of the Kingdom*, *Oxenfree*, *Horizon: Zero Dawn*, *CONTROL*, and *Journey*.

The idea of "what draws me to a game" is interesting. In ways, I am drawn to the same quality in games as I would be in any other form of entertainment—i.e., excellent storytelling! The fundamentals of good writing are the same across any narrative format: you want a well-structured, well-paced narrative that engages with the central themes of the work in thoughtful ways, with well-rounded and dynamic characters and excellent dialogue to boot. But I am also always excited by games that can play with the unique hallmarks and conventions of this format to elicit unique responses.

I think often of the multiplayer feature in the 2012 video game *Journey*, which allows you to run into real-life, anonymous players who are making their way up the mountain at the same time as you are. There are moments of the game you cannot get past without making a connection with someone else, whose presence quite literally strengthens and guides you when you're unable to go on. It's brilliant to use the multiplayer format to underscore the need for connection, empathy, and community, and to signal those as imperative to success even when on a solitary mission for one's own personal benefit. I found it, and continue to find it, incredibly moving.

B: What's a favorite memory of yours of playing a game?

Jocelyn: I grew up in a big family without a traditional video gaming console (unless you count V-Tech's SOCRATES: The Educational Gaming System, which most, including me, would not). We did have PC games, but only one PC, so I have fond memories of all of my sisters and me crowding around our computer as we watched our eldest sister play through a game. The happy accident of this is that I came to associate gaming with conventional entertainment from an early age: I think I see gaming as synonymous to film and television because, in my experience, it always has been! Engaging with games in this manner showed me that games can be as thrilling, involving, and moving as any film or television show (in some cases, more so).

Some of my favourite moments have been of pure gaming satisfaction after completing a difficult task—I think the scream I let out after finally beating Mr. Freeze in *Batman: Arkham City* is still ringing around certain hemispheres. But I also think of moments that have really surprised and moved me. It's a sadder moment, but the final conversation between Lee and Kenny in my playthrough of Telltale's *The Walking Dead: Season One* stuck with me for weeks. Since that game is all about the subtle choices you make having a reverberating effect through the narrative, I was forced to mourn the loss of a friend through choices I had had to make—choices made with the best of intentions, but which fundamentally hurt in ways I could not help or ever atone for. The realization that things between us could never be fixed was so simple in its execution but so profound in its impact, and it moves me to this day to think about it.

B: What got you interested in doing a film and television review podcast and how has your thinking about film, and art in general, changed? How has hosting a film and television podcast affected how you think about games?

Jocelyn: I've wanted to be a writer since I first used our PC to write a poem about *Star Trek: The Next Generation* at the age of 5 (really). I'm never not thinking about film and television, not just because I find it fun and interesting, but because I believe it is imperative to engage thoughtfully with the art we consume. Making a podcast was an intuitive next step for me!

I don't think that making a podcast has changed my feelings about film, games, or art in general. I was very fortunate to go to school and get a bachelor and master's degree in film studies, and I think a lot of the learning and thinking around film and television started there, followed by 6 years of working in professional comedy and 10 years of working as a professional writer. But I do think that my feelings about film and art are always in flux. As we age, meet new people, and accrue different life experiences, our feelings about art—and the feelings they elicit in us—change. Sometimes we understand things more deeply, sometimes we're less willing to accept certain narrative tropes or conventions, sometimes we see things with nuance we weren't able to before. I hope I'm always able to engage thoughtfully with what I'm consuming, and I hope to always be aware of the ways that my feelings are growing and changing with time and with life experience.

B: Much is made of how video games, especially AAA titles, relate to movies and TV. How do you think these media should be similar or different in form and subject matter?

Jocelyn: It's understandable to compare video games to movies and television, but video games share a lot more in common with literature to me – there is a feeling of immersion and involvement in either reading a book or playing a game that movies and television do not always replicate.

In general, I am wary of anyone wanting to be prescriptive about how different types of media should operate. The more we say "this form of art should do X" and "this form of art should do Y," the more we limit ourselves! The "I Lied To You" sequence in *Sinners* is brilliant specifically because it explodes our conceptions of what "should" happen in a genre film, or a period piece.

I agree with Sondheim's rule that "content dictates form." I don't believe there should be any hard and fast rules about what video games should or should not be—whatever they "should be" should be informed by the story they are telling. A game like *The Longing*, for example, is unusual in the sense that it literally takes 400 days to play, but the point of the game is to experience the flow of time, the emotions it invokes in you, and the choices you make as a result. A game like *The Gardens Between* uses an unusual mechanic that's about progressing/reversing the flow of time to solve puzzles, but that mechanic is meant to reflect the way memory works, especially in the context of a long-term friendship: the way we revisit particular moments of our lives, working them over and over again, examining them from different angles as we grow and learn and change. *Batman: Arkham Asylum* uses the fear toxin sequences to collapse the fourth wall—i.e., the famous moment where they use error screens to make you think your entire system has experienced a major breakdown!

B: An idea you come back to talking about movies is satisfaction. How do you think about satisfaction in games being similar or different?

Jocelyn: My idea of satisfaction in film is probably different than most, and I want to be clear that satisfaction does not have to be "a happy ending," "a tidy wrap-up of all narrative threads," or anything implying ease, resolution, or comfort. Satisfaction in film and television, to me, looks like a story well told; a thought well articulated; an idea that's been explored intelligently and with depth.

Satisfaction in gaming is slightly different, because the medium revolves around accomplishment. As I mentioned above, satisfaction often comes from completing a really challenging boss battle, finding the last collectibles you need to get an achievement, etc.

B: What is it you enjoy most about the things you review? What are you always on the lookout for?

Jocelyn: I'm not on the lookout for one particular thing, and I also don't have one particular thing that I could say I enjoy most. I'm curious in general about all forms of media and having fulfilling experiences in each!

B: If you could get any movie or show adapted to a game (digital or tabletop), which would it be and what would that look like? What game would you like to see on film?

Jocelyn: I'm eagerly anticipating the *Zelda* adaptation (if it ever happens), and continue to wish to be hired for a *Portal* adaptation! The *Indiana Jones* game has also been a lot of fun so I would happily see more adaptations of that.

BIBLIOGRAPHY

"About." I Hate It But I Love It, From Superheroes Network, hatelovepodcast.com/about. Accessed 16 March 2026.

Aldrich, Jef, and Jon Taylor. "Red Box Dungeons & Dragons." YouTube, www.youtube.com/watch?v=9Ja3ItX8GIU. Accessed 21 March 2026.

Barbet, Raoul, and Koch, Michel. *Life Is Strange*. Square Enix, PlayStation 4, 2015.

Baumbach, Noah. *The Squid and the Whale*. American Empirical Pictures, United States, 2005.

"BlizzConline 2021 – Where It All Started: The Blizzard Arcade Collection." Blizzard Entertainment. YouTube, www.youtube.com/watch?v=zrrF0JHENGI&t=460s. Accessed 16 March 2026.

Bohl, Robert. *Misspent Youth*. 2nd ed. Robert Bohl Games, United States, 2017.

Bohl, Robert. *Misspent Youth: Sell Out with Me*. Robert Bohl Games, United States, 2017.

Bohl, Robert. *Misspent Youth: Fall In Love, Not in Line*. Robert Bohl Games, United States, 2022.

"Cyberpunk Reflections (Mike Pondsmith & Brian Crecente)." YouTube, Gamelab, www.youtube.com/watch?v=OGCxntJ2pLo. Accessed 21 March 2026.

Dead Kennedys. "In God We Trust, Inc." United States, 1981.

Flesser, Simon. *Sayonara Wild Hearts*. Annapurna Interactive, Nintendo Switch, 2019.

Goldman, Vivien. *Revenge of the She-Punks: A Feminist Music History from Poly Styrene to Pussy Riot*. University of Texas Press, United States, 2019.

Klepek, Patrick. "'Sayonara Wild Hearts' Is a Brilliant, Beautiful Celebration of Pop Music." Vice, 18 Sept. 2019, https://www.vice.com/en/article/sayonara-wild-hearts-is-a-brilliant-beautiful-celebration-of-pop-music/.

Miller, Frank. *Batman: The Dark Knight Returns*. 1st ed. DC Comics, United States, 1986.

Nishikawa, Tomonari. *Market Street*. San Francisco Arts Commission, United States, 2005.

Norbez, Naomi. "Cyberpunk: Writing for Tomorrow – SFWA – the Science Fiction & Fantasy Writers Association." SFWA, 10 July 2025, www.sfwa.org/2021/07/27/cyberpunk-writing-for-tomorrow/.

Otomo, Katsuhiro. *Akira*. Toho, Japan, 1989.

Petro, George, and Haeger, Jack. *Revolution X*. Acclaim Entertainment, United States, 1994.

Regan, Tom. "'It Fully Altered My Taste in Music': Bands Reflect on the Awesome Power of the Tony Hawk's Pro Skater Soundtracks." *The Guardian*, Guardian News and Media, 11 July 2025, www.theguardian.com/games/2025/jul/11/music-tony-hawks-pro-skater-soundtracks.

"Revolution X – Aerosmith – Videogame by Midway Games." Museum of the Game, www.arcade-museum.com/Videogame/revolution-x-aerosmith. Accessed 24 March 2026.

Rollins, Henry. *"Foreward." Punk Rock: An Oral History*, PM Press, Oakland, California, 2006, pp. xi–xiii.

Romano, Aja. "Hopepunk, the Latest Storytelling Trend, Is All about Weaponized Optimism." Vox, 27 Dec. 2018, www.vox.com/2018/12/27/18137571/what-is-hopepunk-noblebright-grimdark.

"Sayonara Wild Hearts." Simogo, https://simogo.com/work/sayonara-wild-hearts/.

Scott, Ridley. *Blade Runner.* Warner Bros, United States, 1982.

Vecchitto, Dan. *Trombone Champ.* Holy Wow Studios, United States, 2022.

CHAPTER 5

Now You're Playing Truth to Power

Neorealism and Documentary

Any good film school student (just kidding, there are no good film school students) will tell you the first documentary was *Nanook of the North*. To a viewer sensitive to the ongoing history of native peoples and the crimes colonizers and occupiers commit against them, the movie oscillates between cringe worthy and laughable. One of the funny moments is when the family is introduced. Nanook gets out of his kayak, which I'll remind you is not open like a canoe, and then his wife and their several children clamber out of the boat. It's hard to tell if this was just economical filmmaking or a sort of clown car joke. Either way, it doesn't play well considering it's real people.

This is all to say that documentaries being "truthful" is spurious. Filmmakers have to edit, so some meaning, some context, and some events are going to get manipulated. I'm not saying that's a problem. Neutrality isn't a virtue, and there's no good argument against documentaries having bias; they just shouldn't present bias as fact. Journalists owe their audiences factuality, with as little adornment as possible, before cutting to commercial. Artists have every right to fill in blanks and get the gist of things. Even memoirists have to make up some of their own lives.

DOI: 10.1201/9781003755821-5

When I was in grad school, some of my classmates argued there couldn't be such a thing as a documentary game. Neither my professors nor my classmates who made documentaries argued thus, but I would guess a lot of people would agree games cannot be nonfiction. It's not an indefensible position, but it doesn't hold up in the context of nonfiction art's history. Even straightforward docs, like Frederick Wiseman's *High School*, have to manipulate footage and employ artificiality. Video games have to produce images through animation, but so do documentaries.

The best argument against games being nonfiction is their feedback interactivity. They change through play. But games have only so many substantive permutations: a game about the economics of roller coasters isn't going to spontaneously offer theories on the Zapruder film. And nonfiction doesn't exist solely to tell stories about "real" people (to differentiate them from actors, who are not real). I would count Stan Brakhage's films as documentaries because, even though they're lyrical and "experimental," they aren't staged or scripted. There's no reason a game about navigating a castle or recreating the sounds of a dead language has to involve specific, fictional characters.

Even though nonfiction art doesn't have "rules," it still has best practices. I love the way Bill Nichols frames it in *Introduction to Documentary* (13–18):

- I (author) speak about them (subjects) to you (audience).
- It (the apparently unauthored film) speaks about them or it to us.
- I or We speak about us to you.

Each is useful for different circumstances. Games like *SimCity* and *Prison Architect* have points of view (an "I"), but they don't include city planners or assistant wardens ("them") on their design teams. Educational games are good examples of "it" speaking about "them," especially if "it" is something like arithmetic or the life cycle of a butterfly. The last is the author within the subject group and in which the group has a voice.

As mentioned in chapter one, *Never Alone* is a strong example of a team of artists platforming people's stories by following the Iñupiat subjects' lead. A more direct example of "we speak about us to you" is *Umurangi Generation*, a photography-based science fiction game by Tali Faulkner, a solo Maōri developer from the Ngāi Te Rangi iwi nation ("Talking"). In an interview with the Indie Game Website, Faulkner talked about coming Respectful Design, a school of thought moving away from Western/human-centric design:

> Respectful Design is by Dr Norm Sheehan. He is an Aboriginal Designer from Australia. I can't really explain respectful design in a sentence because it is sort of an entire philosophy of design that goes along with it. Where I think it departs most from traditional design is that it says agency is with a community, not the designer who comes in. For this game, the players (the community) decide how they want to take photos and what is a good photo, not the game (the design).
>
> *("Talking")*

Rather than using membership as license, Faulkner considers his communities in his work. While the game is certainly science fiction-flavored (alien invaders and giant robots), the care around its concerns and themes makes it feel more real and immediate than many more "realistic" games: "The UN, the big institutional newspapers, the film and advertising industry, they're all inattentive (at best) or hostile (at worst) to the needs of the people threatened by the game's big crisis…It's realistic, because the world has a point of view. Too many other games ignore this" (Klimentov). *Umurangi Generations*' honesty at least flirts with the realm of nonfiction, however apocalyptic.

A lot of games are about the world ending: the whole world, someone else's, just your own. I've been interested in games and memoir for a long time, partly because games contain so, so much death. I don't say that to be morbid. Mario is going to fall down a bottomless pit or get stepped on by a giant winged turtle more times than he's going to rescue Princess Peach. Games ask players to develop a tolerance of failure and frustration, which are two phenomena most memoirists know intimately.

My interest in the memoir/travelogue genre outside of prose began with Guy Delisle's *Pyongyang: A Journey in North Korea*. I was thrilled to find a comic memoir, which led me to titles like Marjane Satrapi's *Perseloplis* and Alison Bechdel's *Fun Home*. These books' daring honesty primed me to understand Anna Anthropy's game *Dys4ia* as a poetic memoir. In *Dys4ia*, players tumble through *WarioWare*-style vignettes about Anthropy's gender transition. It got me thinking about other possibilities for memoir games, including my aborted first MFA thesis project (which I guess makes it an "impossibility").

Later, when I started taking university students on international programs, I needed an angle for my classes. I had recently read a couple of comic travelogues (*Tokyo Travel Sketchbook* and *Tokyo on Foot*) and decided I'd theme the trip around game travelogues. The first time I ran the program, I wrote my single-player poetry RPG, *City the Mouthful.* The structure of the game mirrors my trip through Tokyo and Kyoto and has players searching for a semi-fictional canned coffee. Through play, people generate tanka poems (like haiku, but longer) about loneliness and grief; obsessing over canned coffee was how I distracted myself when I was alone in Japan a few months after my mother died (Figure 5.1).

Anyway, it's a pretty cool game.

FIGURE 5.1 A parody of the Bandai Namco logo, photo by the author.

Speaking of turning millennial malaise into a game, the game memoirs *Perfect Tides* and its sequel, *Perfect Tides: Station to Station* are dedicated to making people around my age wince in recognition ("Oh, god, no, don't act like I used to!" raves A.V. Clubs' William Hughes). The *Perfect Tides* series is helmed by Meredith Gran, cartoonist-author of *Octopus Pie*, and follows the totally not-Meredith Gran protagonist, Mara Whitefish. The first game covers the year she turns 16 while living with her mother and brother on Fire Island, NY. The second follows her to college in "New York City, 2003. Julian Casablancas is God and Karen O is the Virgin Mary. Pitchfork writers both command more respect than the city's mayor and are just as reviled. Young people aren't just anxious over a war unfolding in the Middle East, but also over whether or not The Matrix Reloaded can possibly live up to its predecessor. The internet still feels like a friend" (Colantonio). Much to my chagrin, "Forever wars" in the Middle East and *Matrix* sequels continue to disappoint with a teenager's vicious indifference.

The *Tides* games are, in gamey parlance, "point-and-click adventures," a style popularized in the early days of PC gaming by LucasArts games like 1986's *Maniac Mansion*. Point-and-click games have never been my thing: as soon as I realized *Perfect Tides* was one, I had flashbacks to Sega Genesis' inscrutable *Scooby-Doo Mystery* (the game contains more than one mystery). I should say, *Tides* does not offend my sensibilities as outrageously as the subgenre's classics: turning a sheaf of bubble wrap into a beer cozy is nowhere near as obtuse as whatever the hell was going on in *Leisure Suit Larry*'s puzzles. It's just not my jam.

That doesn't stop me from recognizing *Perfect Tides* perfectly communicates what it felt like to come of age around the year 2000, especially since I suffered some of the same (self-inflicted) indignities as Mara. Her narration opens the game by explaining that the new millennium technically didn't start until the year 2001, and people don't like being thus corrected. I very well may have done that, and if not that specifically, something comparable. There were also benign flashes of recognition. I also had anime posters in my bedroom and a mother who was heartbroken by Diana, Princess of Wales' death. Down to the AOL Instant Messenger startup ritual, *Perfect Tides* nailed the feeling of being a kid in not-quite the new millennium.

I'm glad Meredith Gran and other people are making art about that time, partly because I think back to it and I'm amazed by how weird things were as the 90s ended. I doubt any high school history class would get far enough to talk about the beginning of the Internet, Clinton's impeachment or the September 11 attacks. Even if they did, they wouldn't be able to express how anxious and thrilling it was to be alive then. For Mara, and myself, the Internet was a digital common for hanging out with friends anywhere. Granted, my best friends were a short car ride away, but when you're 14, that's as good as living on an island.

Gran argues that it's specificity that gives people something to which they can relate. "I hope in the telling of it, I am reminding people of their own experiences and, you know, kind of inspiring them to think about it... that this is a way to actually be heard and maybe engage in some sort of collective therapy with other people about this particular period in your life" ("Adapting Life"). Even if chatting online and liking anime didn't take up an outsize space in a player's identity, this game will remind them that, yes, they used to care about some things way, way too much. Teenagers have complicated feelings about their families and are scared to death of pretty much any change, even the ones they want. With that fear comes exhilaration. I was happy to visit being a teenager even as *Perfect Tides* reminded me why I don't want to live there.

Perfect Tides: Station to Station takes up Mara's story in 2003, her first year of college, studying writing in Manhattan. This game opens with a Virginia Woolf quote and some second-person commentary: "It's a cliché to begin with a quote. You know this, but you're a fool. Besides, in order to make good work—work that reaches past mere juvenilia—you must expel your stupidest words. All one million of them. Put them down, so they may die." I don't think opening with a quote is necessarily foolish, but Mara quotes Woolf on the heart "committing its burden to some sea." Given that Woolf committed suicide by weighing herself down and walking into a lake, it feels intentionally foolish to open a story with those words over the tide coming in. "But," asks my inner college student, "how else will the professor know how smart you are?"

While players can definitely start with *Station to Station*, taking the two games together shows the core difference between "mere juvenilia" and the kind of things people write when they're just smart enough to know their writing is bad. In *Tides*, Mara muses on the island's land reclamation program with too-true-to-be-useful insight: "It's a complicated matter, and with all complicated matters, incremental change is all anyone can hope to expect. Sure enough, the erosion has gotten incrementally worse." When asked about *Station to Station*'s narrator being an older, wiser Mara, Gran said, "I don't see the narrator as somebody who is actually capable of being more mature and knowing than Mara. But she certainly believes herself to be so" ("Adapting Life").

Part of what's interesting about comparing the two games is how much more people documented their lives in those three years. It strikes me as funny to animate and fictionalize a time when teens would post "entire albums of terrible, blurry photos from a single night out, write nonstop on LiveJournal, produce appalling juvenilia and then post it on fanfic or art forums" (MacDonald). But rather than relying on ephemera from the aughts, *Station to Station* meticulously recreates the look and feel in fantastic animation.

Which raises the question of whether Meredith Gran's games about Mara Whitefish can properly be called memoirs. Gran herself reserves the right to distance herself from *Tides* with the yardstick of invention, but other artists avowedly make memoirs from that slight distance. Alison Bechdel redrew photos of her family in *Fun Home*, so that narrows the fictive gap. On the other hand, in her book *Spent*, Bechdel casts herself as Alison Bechdel, comic memoirist whose work has been adapted into a prestige TV show starring Aubrey Plaza. It has something to do with dragons. Honestly, it sounds like a pretty great show, even if it stymies the less-real Bechdel.

Comics authors Guy Delisle and Scott McCloud stylize themselves in their books and that does little to break down "memoir-ness." Art Spiegelman's *Maus* goes into the constantly visualized and fictionalized 1940s to chronicle both Spiegelman's father's life as a European Jew and Spiegelman making the comic itself. *Maus* portrays Jews as mice, Germans as cats, and Poles as pigs, but that doesn't make his book a fictitious fable. Then again, it's hard to imagine wanting to argue semantics vis a vis a Holocaust narrative. Then again, again, people have wondered aloud to me why anyone would want to make a comic book about something so awful, so maybe someone would be willing to respond to *Maus* with "well, actually..."

Including all these works in memoir might seem very permissive, but I don't think it is. As Gran puts it, "This isn't a true story. These aren't real people. It is the truth to me because it feels like the truth. But don't try to piece together the details. You will not get the truth by doing that. You will get the truth by accepting the story that I'm telling" ("Adapting Life"). Saying memoir is about "a feeling of truthfulness" is actually demanding.

Fargo claims to be based on a true story, and that's just a lie. It's a funny enough gag on its own, but in the context of other Hollywood movies "based on" true stories, the joke feels honest. I was once asked, while talking about Spielberg's *Lincoln*, if I wanted "truth" in the movies I watched. Honest Abe was played by method acting madman Daniel Day-Lewis, so maybe they had a point, but a movie like that isn't documentary: it's hagiography.

Realness' value depends on whether it makes a work of art more honest, but "real" is on a slider anyways, which makes neorealism so useful. The film school syllabus' go-to example is Vittorio De Sica's *Bicycle Thieves*. Set in destitute postwar Italy, *Bicycle Thieves* is about a poor father who gets a bicycle for a job. It gets stolen, and he and his son look for it. Not a complicated story, but complication isn't sophistication. The movie's power comes from its rawness: it was shot on location with amateur actors. Everyone and everything look ready to fall over.

It's not a documentary. They're fictional characters in a believable situation, one that almost certainly happened, but the movie doesn't point to that. It hardly points to its characters being persons. It's a deeply felt film, but not because the father and son are specific and well-drawn characters. A more fictitious film would load the father and son with quirks and some emotional tension to resolve at the end. It wouldn't have to be a happy ending, but it would need a resolution. *Bicycle Thieves* isn't that kind of movie. It lays out what a documentary about that time and place might look like.

This War of Mine, a survival game, takes the perspective of civilians during war. In *This War*, players take on the role of a "group of civilians trying to survive in a besieged city; struggling with lack of food, medicine and constant danger from snipers and hostile scavengers" ("This War"). It's generally understood to be inspired by accounts of the Battle of Sarajevo, though it seems any corroborating websites are dead. There are plenty of conflicts which could have inspired this video game.

When the game starts, players control a character sharing a house with other survivors. In the "day cycle," players manage typical chores like cooking along with clearing rubble from the house and repairing rooms to a habitable condition. The characters have mental health along with their physical health, so they need distraction and recreation. In my playthrough, one of the men living in my house had depression so acute he killed himself. The "night cycle" is, as one would expect, harrowing: "survival horror" taken to a realistic extreme. I had to defend my house from robbers, which meant shooting them to death. *This War of Mine* is shocking and sobering because the violence is, in no way, fun.

The un-fun of *This War*'s violence isn't the only thing different. In the game, as in real life, violence looks and feels clumsy and messy. More importantly, violence doesn't function on most players' expectations of game rules. While scavenging for food, my character broke into a building and found an elderly couple living there. I had a weapon, but I didn't want to kill an old man, so I thought I'd just punch him and be on my merry way. I've played so many games over the years in which there are a handful of nonlethal options, so I assumed that was the case here. Imagine my surprise when I found out I beat the old man to death over some tinned tuna. I ran through the kinds of questions movies teach us to ask ourselves at such times. "Am I a monster? Am I any better than the killers I hate?" Ultimately, it didn't matter if my character was the same as any of the soldiers murdering people in the street. My character survived.

This War holds game conventions at arm's length so the player has to take a good look. The game is functionally 2D, with all action taking place on one plane viewed in profile. The camera is positioned about ten yards from the player character, creating an emotional distance between the player and their sense of accomplishment or failure. Each survivor's character sheet has an actual photo, so players do know what they look like, but the interface reminds you that you aren't looking at people. You're looking at pictures of people.

A lot of games have morality systems or evaluate player behavior in some way beyond "performed well/poorly." *BioShock*'s good/evil system has players decide whether or not to kill little girls (in all fairness, they are kind of weird looking). I played the game when it was new and when a character told me I'd get rewarded down the line if I didn't kill the little girls, I believed her. Granted, that was me believing a former Nazi scientist, but I knew the game wasn't going to lie to me. It was simply not how video games operated. In *This War of Mine*, goodness isn't rewarded. Orphans might show up at a player's door begging for food when really, they're casing the player's house. But then again, maybe not! Even if the orphans just want whatever food you'll give them, they won't reward you. That's fairy tale logic.

There is also, and I was surprised to find this out, a *This War of Mine* board game. It is, apparently, a faithful recreation of the video game with lots of bits and bobs to track resources and progress. I bring it up because I came across a BoardGameGeek.com review by a player, Jasenko Pasic, who purportedly survived the Siege of Sarajevo. (I have no reason or inclination to doubt the veracity; I just can't confirm it.) This person was a child at the time and offered a tremendous account of why a board game is an entirely appropriate medium for digging into life in a war zone.

"When I was 8 years old the Siege of Sarajevo began. It lasted until I was 12. Even though those times were terrible, if you ask me about the siege, and don't dig enough inside me, I will tell you just about how great those times were," writes Pasic. While he "never had that much fun," people took care of each other. "But, if you dig deep enough..."

> War brings out the best and the worst from people. There were some terrible people in Sarajevo during the siege. They had everything whilst others had nothing. I found trading the most stressful part of the game. My dad had once traded a TV for a pack of cigarettes and few eggs. That is how life is. But that is a subject for another time. People can be amazingly good, and unthinkably terrible.
>
> This is an impressive game. It is more than a game. I know how every game is supposed to be an experience, but with this one you really get one. I am, often, asked 'How was it, living under the siege?'. Talking about it does not do it justice. From now on, if I get that question, I'll sit down and play a round or two with ones who asks.

Pasic begs off any authority of writing a review ("I will not go deep into how game plays as there are a lot of more skilled people on BGG"), but I'm with the comments section in lauding this honesty and vulnerability.

What I appreciate most about *This War* on a design level is how it frames success and failure. A player doesn't win or lose; their characters survive or die. It's evaluative, not judgmental, feedback which lets players explore their experiences with more open minds. Failure is worth exploring because everyone does it sometimes, and games in general benefit when they make failure more interesting. In heroic stories, heroes win even if they die: the story existing is a victory. If we want to think about how normal people survive and die, it's more honest to look at every reason why and how things shook out the way they did. It reminds me of this conversation from *Maus* between Art Spiegelman and his therapist Pavel, who also survived the camps.

Pavel: So, do you admire your father for surviving?
Spiegelman: Well… sure. I know there was a lot of luck involved, but he was amazingly present-minded and resourceful…
P: Then you think it's admirable to survive. Does that mean it's not admirable to not survive?
S: Whoosh. I-I think I see what you mean. It's as if life equals winning, so death equals losing.
P: Yes. Life always takes the side of life, and somehow the victims are blamed. But it wasn't the best people who survived, nor did the best ones die. It was random! (204-5)

That's true, but the murder of millions and millions of Jews, communists, Roma, and queer people was also heavily systematized. Artists need to view the world clearly ("It was random!") but also have to do something with that observation.

The other day, I was talking with some students about a game they were working on. It was about a landlord and tenants and, despite the designers "nerfing" (weakening) the landlord twice, the tenants kept losing. One of the designers shrugged and said maybe it should just be kept this way because it was realistic. I acknowledged that, yes, it is more realistic for tenants to get screwed, but that is no great revelation. Asking some players to wallow in penury and another to revel in their abjection is so *boring*. There's value in pointing out what we already know: if we aren't all having the same social conversation, we're not even arguing. Even so, art is more interesting when it has an answer to "so what?"

The artfulness of documentary and neorealism is how they contextualize how we live now and can indicate better ways to live. Of course, it was difficult for students to design a game evenly balanced between landlords and tenants. They've never seen it in real life, and that makes it seem inevitable. "I think hard times are coming, when we will be wanting the voices of writers who can see alternatives to how we live now, and see through our fear-stricken society," said Ursula K. LeGuin on her acceptance of an award for her contributions to American literature. She described these artists as "the realists of a larger reality" who "recognized the difference between the production of a commodity and the practice of an art." To her mind, capitalism and capitalists' obsession with technology were the enemy to better ways of living, which is truer today than it was in 2014. She acknowledged what my students discovered, that capitalism seems "inescapable." But, LeGuin pointed out "so too did the divine right of kings."

LeGuin said the ideas that change the world for the better often start in art. I think she's correct, and of course it makes sense that sentiment would come from a novelist and poet who worked in science fiction and fantasy. Nonfiction, documentary, and realist storytelling take a different, if closely related, kind of imagining. I've heard often enough that there are optimists, pessimists, and realists, but that just isn't true. People either work to make the future better by caring for their families and communities, or they don't do the work. If a realist (of a smaller reality) is not someone who sees the world as it is because the world is always changing. Being an optimist isn't ignoring what the world is like. Being an optimist is doing the work to make the world a more just place.

Carly Dwyer is a game designer, educator, and head of Intramersive, a theatrical live-action roleplaying game company. Her popular *Daemonologie* series focuses on social themes and spooky monsters.

B: Talk to me a bit about what your games are, what they're like, what it looks like when people play them.

Carly: Sure. So our games are speculative histories where we have a cast of characters who are like the NPCs of the game and are played by professional actors. We have audience members buy tickets. Some people know what they're getting into. Some people don't. It's usually around 40 people per show and they're invited into the world of these characters.

They're given maybe a 15-minute onboarding telling them anything they need to know about the historical period, the essential things they need to know about the characters, and also how the audience fits into the world, like "you're all benefactors coming to a charity ball. You're all here to witness a seance." And then they meet these characters in that context. Usually, the moment of action happens where the story starts to feel like the world we've built falls apart a bit. Then the real problems we're dealing with come out.

Characters spread out across the house or the property, and scenes start to happen simultaneously as everyone is trying to deal with the situation in real time. Audience members fit into the world automatically. They're accepted as is. No one questions. There's none of that obnoxious, Plymouth Plantation, "What is that strange box you hold?" They interact with the characters as the characters are trying to figure out their problems.

Players oftentimes are sent to go find out information or check on a noise. Players can come and go from scenes as they please, but they can't see the whole show at once. They can't get all the information. And as the players play through their arcs, we come to points of the story where the characters can no longer help themselves, and that usually turns into a large group debate where the audience are the only people who can come up with the outcome.

Because the characters are so deeply invested, they cannot get out of this on their own. The audience then deliberates, usually with one character as kind of the moderator. While they're deliberating, we [the Intramersive team] are listening in, and we are devising an ending based on what players are saying. And then they, the actors will come in, tell players what their fate is, and they will play through an ending.

B: Talk to me about how Intramersive uses history and nonfiction.

Carly: They're cheats. First, because we especially wanted to get players to come play our games who are not dedicated gamers. We didn't want to appeal just to LARPers, we wanted regular people to experience the fun of immersive play. Sure. And the hardest thing, in my opinion, about doing that with people off the street is getting them to buy in.

The idea of designing a whole world was like, "Oh my God, we're going to teach this to them, and they're gonna have questions." And it's just, it's too much. We cannot invent the whole world. But we couldn't do it contemporary because then you get a whole bunch of people who are fact checking you on their phones and that's super freaking annoying.

So we kind of came into the history aspect because people feel like they know enough about history, but they're usually very excited to find out things were different than they thought they were. And also, we're very much more willing to believe in fantastical elements about history than we are to believe about in our contemporary time. No one's going to argue with you about how magic works.

If you do a modern magic piece, people are going to pull in their own knowledge and then suddenly you're arguing different magic systems for different fandoms. If you put it in the Puritans' time, it's just so much easier. You know, you can have magic at the seance table in the 19th century. It's so much easier. So on the one hand, you can get the audience into a world they are familiar enough with but then play along with we're going to ask them. And honestly, we found the easiest thing to do was just do more research because our perceptions of history are usually incredibly wrong.

And so, if we wanted to introduce magic into the world, we didn't have to invent anything. We just had to go back and do deeper digging into the accounts written by the people in those times.

B: What does that onboarding you mentioned look like?

Carly: We usually break it down to three parts. The first part is what our shows are going to look like, and we are really deliberate about telling people what to expect. We've learned over the years that particularly audiences in Boston do not like surprises. They like to know exactly what's going to happen.

So we tell them, "You're about to go into this room, you're going to meet all of our characters. We'll talk about them in a minute. They're going to do a presentation. And once they leave, follow whomever you like." We tell them, "Don't touch them." We go over touching rules, safety rules. We tell them not to touch artifacts in the museums that we're usually working in.

We go over kind of the way the players are allowed to interact in the world, the expectations of safety, the expectations of play. We then talk about the historical context of the world, like, "The world you're walking into is 1950. And at this time in Salem, these are the key, important things you need to know. We're five years after World War II, and Salem was more invested in that than you think. U-boats were spotted off the coast. Those lighthouses out there? They were U-boat watchers, they spotted U-boats, and they didn't tell anybody. They weren't allowed to.

"The teenagers who used to work at this house… this was a haven for immigrants learning to work, and working in community, to kind of assimilate and get into American culture."

We give the context of, "Here's the broad view of the world; here's how the city we're in is affected by it. Here's how the people living in this house are affected by it. And now here are our characters." And so all of that boils down to, "Tonight you're at a fundraiser to help the women who run Settlement House, the social workers. You'll see, one of their great benefactors is here. And she's interested in raising funds for the Science Museum, so you're going to meet them."

And then we send them in. We try to keep that to about 15 minutes because people get antsy. So yeah, we try to keep that tight. And every single night we figure out what didn't read from the history side or the player side. We adjust.

B: What does that research actually look like?

Carly: It's so many primary sources. That gets harder when you get back into things like the body snatching at Harvard University, which happened in the 17th century. That was a lot harder to find.

How the research usually works is we create the outline of the story we're interested in telling. We want to talk about, you know, kaiju crabs in the nuclear age of the 1950s. We want to talk about body snatching and medical practices in the 17th century, in the years leading up to the writing of *Frankenstein.*

We want to talk about spiritualism in Salem the year before the passing of the Fugitive Slave Act, when Salem's populations is extremely diverse. Like, these are the things we want to talk about. Okay. Who are the main characters who get involved with that? Here are the characters that would be most involved in that.

Then we try to ask, "Who do we want to be an actual historical person?" versus, "Who do we want to be a composite?" All of our fictional characters are always composites of real people. We're doing our best to represent people from their time as authentically as we can. We try to avoid historical characters, especially in the 1950s because of living memory. In fact, we had women from Settlement come to our show who are still doing social work. They loved it.

Salem's Settlement is one of the last Settlement houses left in America, which are houses run by women, female social workers, who were about taking in immigrant populations and helping them learn English, helping them learn job skills, providing them daycare, providing them after school programs, school support, you know, community support. The one we worked with is one of the last left in America. And it was one of the first. So it's the oldest and longest running, and they have an incredible tradition. They don't work in the House of the Seven Gables anymore, but they are still an active Settlement House.

And so we're doing the 1950s, which was a very interesting period for the Settlement House in terms of their mission changing because of the war. We're in our own period right now of their work with immigration being extremely important and dangerous.

We wanted to make sure we were representing them well and respectfully while also doing a show about, you know, giant monster crabs. We didn't want to base those women on anyone in particular, because we weren't sure if any of them are still alive and doing this work. So we made composites that we hoped people could recognize. And when the women of Settlement came and did our show, they had such a good time. They were actually really excited to see that. We used a lot of their archival materials in the show; they were really excited about how we talked about their work.

They loved the characterization of the women and the way the women, our characters, talked about their work. They said all of it really read true. They also just loved the sci-fi crabs. They were all about the super-crabs.

B: When you say that, at some point in the evening, the center won't hold and the real problems start coming out, what does that look like in different games and shows you've run?

Carly: Usually that's the moment that the supernatural enters the show. And we use the supernatural largely as an alibi to talk about bigger social issues that are either too complex to do justice to in this setting, or too hot topic to do in this setting without creating unsafe conditions. And often a lot of the periods we're looking at are known for their supernatural element because the supernatural is how people address their problems. The one we did about spiritualism in 1849, they're doing a fake, tricked-up seance where they're using table knockers and things like that. And it turns out the girl really is possessed. And she's being exploited, and she's an Irish servant who barely survived coffin ships, and she's an orphan in this country.

Her future is incredibly precarious. And so the fact that she is also possessed, you know, is the question of whether the man she's working for is actually trying to help her, or is he exploiting her? Is she capable? Becoming a famous medium could be her ticket to independence. She doesn't have to be a maid anymore. But does she have control over this? Is this what she wants? How do you trust her consent in a situation where the options are destitution and dying on the street? So usually the point where the facade falls apart is when the supernatural enters the story, when it enters that chaotic, unknowable moment where some characters obviously know what's going on and are trying to hide it or control it.

Other characters take a little while to get on board with what's going on. They don't believe it. And we try to spread out the kinds of character reactions to cover everyone in the audience and be like, "I don't believe that these crabs are actually going to be giants," or "I don't believe she's actually possessed." There's someone players can talk to who's with them. Like, for example, Nathaniel Hawthorne coming to the seance. He hated this stuff. Hated it. Thought it was absolute rubbish. And that's interesting because his wife was into spiritualism. She was cool, Sophia was. Anyway, the whole bit of Sophia dragging her husband to the seance is very realistic.

Nathaniel Hawthorne wrote a lot about magic, and he lived in this time, so this is actually something he would have to confront, the fact that Sophia did believe in spiritualism. She and her sisters had seances. They were into it, so he has to deal with the fact that it is impacting the world around him in his own time, and in our play.

Even if you're like, "Well, I don't believe she's possessed," suddenly you're not in the game anymore. But you still are because the possessed girl is still sick. There's still stuff happening and you can disbelieve in the magical all you want, but there's still a problem and a girl is possibly getting trafficked. Deal with it.

B: And the supernatural comes from the time period and reflects their social anxieties, and that kind of thing?

Carly: Right. Like when we did our original show about witch hunting in 1680s, we very much talked about, "What the Puritans actually afraid of?" Because whenever people think about it, they're like, "Oh, they're afraid of women who did herbal magic." And that's not true. That was actually legal. So what were they actually afraid of? What were the things they were hunting down?

And let's just work off of the idea of "what if that were true?" And in that process, we realized how much the dark plays into that. That was an environmental discovery that was huge.

When the dark is always creeping in on you, it does feel, you feel alone in the world and you feel lost. And we realized how much that plays into a sense of paranoia when you're in a land that you don't feel welcome in. That's dark and scary and deadly and you're afraid of the devil. You know it really does feel like the devil is everywhere. Or raccoons. One or the other.

So yeah, we always pull from the magic of the time because the magic of the time tells us what they were afraid of. Even in the 1950s, that was the great age of the monster film and UFOs. People were so afraid of science getting beyond them. So the monsters became the uncontrolled consequences of emboldened science without thinking about the future.

B: What is your design philosophy for an immersive game?

Carly: That's a… okay. It's a tricky question. I have an answer to that. I hope this is helpful. I think the core of building an entire immersive game is we build, I think we build a very good labyrinth of character boundaries and world boundaries.

B: What does that mean?

Carly: So we don't tell the audiences what to think and we don't tell the audiences what the outcome should be. It's like we've built out a labyrinth of multiple, sort of, points. We're always going to get to the center. How you get there is up to you, but it's not chaos because we've built out, you know, a world that is contained within the physical space of the show, a world that is contained within the timeline of the show.

It all happens in real time. That locks us into a set amount of resources, like everything has to stay very realistic and very immediate, and then the characters only know what their characters know; the actors can only talk about what their characters would know. So no one has to be a full expert, and those characters are always acting toward their own character's goals.

You can influence them. We've definitely had characters change sides in shows because audiences play very well, but the motivation has to be like, "Well, I want her, Nora, to be okay. I don't want this demon to possess her anymore. I thought the doctor was the right path, but I've been convinced that it's actually this."

There's a lot of walls set up. Not necessarily to railroad player interactions, but to kind of... if a player's bumping up against something that's just a dead end, there's a really solid reason why they're redirected. And that redirect is self-motivated.

B: Sure. And when you say when the player is doing those interactions, what are the player's things to do?

Carly: The actors are always improvising their dialogs around key points that have to be brought up in that scene. And then we practice ways for them to talk to each other. That gives the impression that they know what they're talking about, but they're not immediately explaining everything to get people to ask questions.

"What is that?"

"Oh well that's this."

They'll start explaining something and--

"Wait, that's really important. What do you mean?"

"I heard knocking outside the window and, oh, well, I didn't think anything of it."

They start like this every single time an audience member scratches the surface, which encourages them to ask more questions.

We'll also design scenes that are emotionally heated. We're really good at casting actors that people really want to engage with. The likability of the actors is so key because then, you know, people will be watching a difficult, emotional scene and a character will always sit down and ask to take someone's hand. And then? They're that player's person. They will ride or die with that character.

So player actions are to provide support, to provide information, and they become advocates. They like and become friends with the characters as and, the more information comes out, the more you realize that the characters cannot fix this. That increases the audience's need to share information and get involved.

B: How does using history and research, basically the nonfiction elements, how does that get players invested in the deliberation at the end?

Carly: I think, again, we accidentally ended up a history company because history is so weird. It's deliciously weird, but it's also made up of incredibly human decisions. So I think when we use the history, when we rely harder on the history and just kind of use narrative wax to connect things and fill in gaps, then like they feel like facts. Because in a lot of ways they are facts. When the audience starts to deliberate, they're pulling from something that feels real.

Like, "I know that how that radio works because it was explained to me and it makes sense. I know what a radio is. So of course that's how this radio works, and I saw it do a thing it wasn't supposed to do. I saw them unplug it from the wall." The more fact-based the show is, and even though the audiences don't always know when we've made something up versus when we haven't, it feels realistic enough for them to become authorities on the subject matter by the time it comes to deliberation.

B: Have you ever tamped down something historical because the nonfiction is, or sounds, too fictive?

Carly: Yes. Yeah. Actually, we ran into that with *Smoke and Mirrors*. The one based in 1849 and was about spiritualism and seances. It was a combination of the influx of Irish immigrants to America from the Great Hunger, the beginnings of the burgeoning textile trades and the Industrial revolution up in Massachusetts, and a year before the Fugitive Slave Act.

Two of our characters came from Louisiana, and they were siblings. One of them was a Black woman, and the other one was a white man, and they were half-siblings. One thing that came up in our research was that there was this tradition of Creole families that owned plantations who (not often, but it happened enough to be a thing), would have a half-Black sibling or a Black sibling who owned a plantation.

That was something we found in the record, and we were talking with the actor who is from from the South and from a Creole family, and we're like, "Hey, is this something that you're interested in?" And they were like, "Yes, I would 100% like to talk about this." And so we designed Delphine around being a plantation-owning black woman.

And audiences had a willful ignorance of that. The actor wanted to talk about it and we tamped it down. The audience just wasn't going to hear it. Yeah. They were not going to hear it. They were not going to hear that Delphine owned people. And it actually became a joke with the actor where every single night Delphine would say something a little more hardcore just to see if the audience would agree with her. Because our audiences are largely white. Delphine would say something that, if it came out of a white person's mouth, you'd immediately know it was racist, but not unexpected for the time period of the show.

Somebody actually did bring up to Delphine one time: "Wouldn't you move up to Canada? Aren't you afraid if they pass the Fugitive Slave Act? Aren't you nervous?"

And Delphine said, "Oh, that happens to poor Black people."

But the audience member said that wasn't it. And audiences just could engage if we brought up like classism or the fact that Delphine was a landowner and thought that protected her. The actor really liked to play with that, to see if she could push audiences to respond to that character. It's kind of the opposite of what you're asking, but we could not get audiences to engage with that.

B: Speaking of engaging players, tell me about *Mirror in Dark Water.*

Carly: Oh, that is a game I wrote, about the Tollund Man, mostly because I've always had a weird, morbid fascination with bog bodies. It's a black box, kind of parlor LARP.

B: What does that mean?

Carly: It's a live action roleplaying game where all the people participating in it are players playing characters that are written for the game, and you can play it in any setting, like a black box theater, a living room, a cabin in Denmark. And it can function in any one of those places. You don't need a special location. Quiet is best, but as I've learned at conventions, it doesn't have to be quiet. So, yeah, it's a LARP that can be played with very few props, very little setting. You don't necessarily need costumes.

Mirror in Dark Water is a character-driven LARP about human sacrifice. It's a thought exercise I came up with after spending a really long time researching the archeological and anthropological studies of, particularly, Tollund man and other bog bodies from that time period.

B: Cool. What's a bog body?

Carly: Okay. A bog body is a human body discovered in a bog. Peat bogs in particular, because the chemistry of a peat bog basically...

> the bog tans and pickles the body, so they are more or less very well preserved. But there is very little evidence on bodies from the Iron Age period of northern Europe. Not a lot of them have defensive wounds. And, contrary to popular belief, they were not high. They were not drunk. They were not unconscious, and there's evidence to show that many of them walked themselves out there, so they weren't killed ahead of time.

Which means those people went with some form of willingness. And we now know, thanks to like isotope studies, that they were from these communities, so they weren't foreigners. They weren't like, to the best of our knowledge, prisoners. Many of them were in good health. So for some reason, these relatively healthy members of their community are allowing themselves to be walked out to bogs and then killed, and there is something very haunting to me about that.

It's easy to think there's some reason these people were disposable and then you think, "What are sacrifices?" You don't sacrifice junk; you sacrifice something of value. And then I thought about what it would be like to live in a society where an act of violence, of murdering your neighbor, can be consensual and an act of love?

Then I thought about what sort of conditions you have to live under, so I started doing more research of what we think their societies were like and I developed a game that is an approach to what a discussion around sacrifice might have looked like among village elders.

They [players] don't have to sacrifice. They generally do, but they try not to. And I think it's fascinating. Yeah.

B: So here's the thing: I would I would argue *Mirror in Dark Water* is a documentary game.

Carly: I'd like to think so. I did a lot of research.

B: So why does that matter? I know why I'm making that distinction and why I care about it being nonfiction. But what does that mean to you?

Carly: Because when you are looking at history, particularly history where we have less access to primary sources or no access to primary sources, like in this case, the body itself is the only primary source we have. It's so easy to lay our values and our own social structures upon them.

B: Sort of like The Crucible, right?

Carly: Yeah. And it's so easy to just make them us. And it's a very tricky line to walk, understanding that we are all interconnected, these people did experience so many things that we experience today like love and fear and all, they had to get up every day and do a job that they probably weren't thrilled about. A lot of them probably worshiped gods that they weren't sure were there. Those are very uniting human forces.

But their social beliefs were different. Their social values were different. And if we rob them of the opportunity to try to tell us who they were, we are missing opportunities to understand more about how we could be or how we got here. For something like *Mirror in Dark Water*, when I was writing it and testing it, one of the tests I did, the people were so focused on having a political marriage. I'm like, "Guys that's not this time period." Most people think it's "castle times, right?" "No, you're a thousand years from castle times." They're thinking it's all chiefdoms and political marriages and that's not it. We didn't even have city states at that point. These are hunter gatherer societies, and some agriculture. Pretty good agriculture, actually. But these are hierarchal, but non-stratified societies.

And when you start chipping away at our biases about these people, you actually have to kind of come to terms with the fact that there is something very sophisticated and something very deeply emotional about this. I will say this is a documentary game. I will also say I'm sure there are researchers out there who would read it and say, "She's picking favorites." Yes, I am. It's a game.

What I love so much about watching people play *Mirror* is, and you've seen it, when people have come to play it: "Teddy, I'm going to put you in the bag, bro." They're joking about it. And then they get into it. They realize that one of these people could die and they're going to have to pick it, and that person has to agree. Then they don't want to do it and they're fighting against it. How do they figure out how to not sacrifice somebody without putting the village at risk?

Then they realize like maybe they do just have to sacrifice somebody. "But what if we kill them and… and the village is still at risk?" And then they are completely at a loss to know if they can control their own destinies. At the same time, someone's life usually ends up getting sacrificed because somebody says, "I will do this for the rest of you." And hot damn, if that doesn't hit every single time.

I think it's beautiful because I think we have a tendency—when you're standing in a museum and you're looking down through glass at somebody who died a horrible, violent death, that looks kind of monstrous, except in the case of Tollund Man, where he's so well preserved—to focus on the brutality and look on those people with disgust. We're doing everybody a disservice.

I'm also trying not to romanticize it. I'm trying to humanize it. They're not worse than us. And let's be real: we all know somebody who would sacrifice themselves for others, and would we let them do it? Would we help them do it? What kind of circumstances do we have to get into for that to even come up?

There's a lot to that. And it did work. We don't know anything about these people. The more we learn from these bodies, the more we learn who these people were. So it did work. These people did immortalize their people.

B: What do people actually do during play?

Carly: My favorite way to do the first half of *Mirror* is gathering for a meal. I think the gathering for a meal works so well because everybody is communally working in a way that they understand: they're working to make a feast together. Feasting is so universal across history, a way that people like to come together. Especially since we're talking about resource management in a largely agrarian society. So everyone sitting down for a meal and talking about the politics of how to survive the winter, and then finishing that meal. Then we jump ahead to the early spring and find out what actually did happen during the winter.

It's usually when everyone's kind of picking over the bones of the meal, like the last couple of grapes. They realize now they're in the time when their resources are diminished, or like however the winter went. Now they have to make decisions going forward because time's still coming. This is a climate that experiences a starvation cycle.

I'd be actually curious to play this game in an equatorial region where they don't have starvation cycles, and they have multiple harvest cycles.

How would people coming from that kind of background understand this type of sacrifice cycle? I'd be really curious to play that.

B: You mentioned that's the first half. What does the second half look like?

Carly: The second half is early spring and whoever's running the game will give the winter report, and everyone gets the update of how their character fared over the winter. How the village fared over the winter, because every character represents a role like farmer or shepherd or blacksmith, and they are the elder of essentially that guild of workers. That was the easiest way to make the game work.

So they all have a state of how they're doing at the end of the winter, and everyone has a piece of expertise to give. Like, "Hey I can't promise you, but I'm pretty sure the spring is going to be really wet. And you know what? Honestly, we did not lose as many elders as we thought we were going to. But we had a huge surge of births because it was a mild winter. So now we're facing overpopulation. We do have surplus. But what if we have a bad harvest?"

We've learned from some of these bodies that sacrifice cycles happened during times of surplus, not during times... I mean you can't afford to sacrifice somebody during times of like struggle. You need all the resources you can get. Which also contradicts what people would think, like, "Oh we have too many mouths to feed. Let's send Bob to the bog." That's not what we see as the pattern of sacrifice, which again is why the research is important. I remember when I was writing the game and I learned that, it was a huge turning point for me because I'm like, "Why would they sacrifice during a time of surplus?"

I had to dig into kind of the anthropology of that. And, again, it changed the game. I think that's actually a huge point in the game for everybody: "Well we're doing so well what could possibly go wrong?" Well, what happens if you cannot maintain this?

Then the third part is, if you don't sacrifice, you have to play a game of chance. Only one group has ever done it. We basically play a game of chance with dice for how the seasons go. You can do a substitute sacrifice, so everyone has to take basically a year's worth of what one human would use in a cycle and sacrifice that to the bog. It's overwhelming when people realize how much material that is, especially realizing that so much of that stuff is used communally. To sacrifice a year's worth of clothes and food and wool and, you know, pots and things like that to the bog is an incredible amount and takes away from everybody.

So, they don't usually end up doing that because they're realizing that sacrificing one person does actually benefit everybody, so then it boils down to you put a person in the bog. That's usually what happens because usually someone volunteers, and there has to be a general consensus. Usually there's somebody who absolutely does not want to do it, and it's brutal.

Then everyone has to play through their ritual. They have to design the ritual that will put their friend in the bog, and they have to perform it to the level that the group is comfortable doing. Originally, when I wrote it, I said, "You're never going to perform the sacrifice. That's too much." Then I realized that's actually part of the anxiety cycle of the game. You have to follow through, and you have to process the feelings of that. It's a lot. Yeah, it's a lot.

But people leave it feeling really good. Someone always cries during it, and yet you come out of it feeling really good, like you really love each other at the end of this game. "We sacrificed our friend, but we all had to give up something that we could all survive." There's an enormous amount of goodwill at the end of this game, which I was surprised at. And I was really really happy about it. But I ran a total bummer of a game.

As an anthropologist and a folklorist, I think documentary gameplay is so incredibly important because you can do fact-based history, but to get people to experience the lives and struggles of others, even in the smallest possible way, builds the empathy I think is so critically important to humanizing the past and other cultures. I think gameplay is unique in that sense.

BIBLIOGRAPHY

Anthropy, Anna. *Dys4ia*. itch.io, 2023.

Bechdel, Alison. *Fun Home: A Family Tragicomic*. Houghton Mifflin, Boston, United States, 2006.

Bechdel, Alison. *Spent: A Comic Novel*. HarperCollins, Boston, United States, 2025.

Coen, Joel. *Fargo*. Working Title Films, United States, 1996.

Colantonio, Giovanni. "Oh god, I feel seen by this playable ode to blog bands and late-night AIM sessions." Polygon, 2026. https://www.polygon.com/perfect-tides-station-to-station-review/

Delisle, Guy. *Pyongyang: A Journey in North Korea*. Drawn & Quarterly, Montreal, Canada, 2003.
De Sica, Vittorio. *Bicycle Thieves*. Produzioni De Sica, Italy, 1948.
Drozdowski, Michał, and Marszał, Przemysław. *This War of Mine*. Base edition. 11 bit studios, Poland, 2014.
Faulkner, Tali. *Umarangi Generation*. Origame Digital, 2020.
Flaherty, Robert J. *Nanook of the North*. Pathé Exchange, 1922.
Gran, Meredith. *Perfect Tides*. Three Bees, 2022.
Gran, Meredith. *Perfect Tides: Station to Station*. Three Bees, 2026.
Klimentov, Mikhail. "'Umurangi Generation': A Photography Game That Urges You to Look Closer." *Washington Post*, www.washingtonpost.com/video-games/reviews/umurangi-generation-photography-game-that-urges-you-look-closer/. Accessed 29 March 2026.
LeGuin, Ursula K. "Ursula K. Le Guin's defense of Art over Profits." Femalepoetssociety, Instagram, htps://www.instagram.com/reel/DL8FKNpi_4y/
Levine, Ken; Finley, Alyssa. *BioShock*. 2k, United States, 2007.
MacDonald, Keza. "Gaming's New Coming-of-Age Genre Embraces 'Millennial Cringe.'" The Guardian, Guardian News and Media, 4 Feb. 2026, www.theguardian.com/games/2026/feb/04/gamings-new-coming-of-age-genre-embraces-millennial-cringe.
Nichols, Bill. *Introduction to Documentary*. Indiana University Press, United States, 2001.
Pasic, Jasenko. "This War of Mine - Review." Board Game Geek. https://boardgamegeek.com/thread/1816826/article/26449801264498O1.
Plante, Chris. "Adapting Life into a Video Game (Meredith Gran)." Post Games, United States, 2026.
Scooby-Doo Mystery. Sega Genesis, Acclaim Entertainment, United States, 1995.
Sichling, Brandon. *City the Mouthful*. https://brandonlsichling.itch.io/city-the-mouthful, United States, 2023.
Spiegelman, Art. *The Complete Maus: A Survivor's Tale*. Pantheon, New York, United States, 1996.
Spielberg, Steven. *Lincoln*. DreamWorks Pictures, United States, 2012.
"Talking Climate Change and Māori Culture with Umurangi Generation." The Indie Game Website, 5 June 2020, www.indiegamewebsite.com/2020/06/05/talking-climate-change-and-maori-culture-with-umurangi-generation/.
"This War of Mine." 11 bit studios., Poland, https://11bitstudios.com/games/this-war-of-mine/
Wiseman, Frederick. *High School*. Grove Press, United States, 1968.

Afterworld

New Game Minus

Artists have always wondered if artwork makes any difference, which is funny because someone else's art mattered to us before we took up the work. It's wild to think our art, then, can't matter. Our reactions to art include a professional bent, but caring about art doesn't make artists special. It's reasonable to worry one's work is not accomplishing what it might, but it is silly to wonder if anything we *could* do is important. It's true, we are not curing cancer in children, but there are lots of ways to save a life. For a lot of people, making art is just paying it forward.

I remind my students (and myself) that if art didn't matter, then it wouldn't be worth censoring. Dictators wouldn't bother lashing out against or co-opting artists and artwork if we didn't have power. There was a time when I would have pointed out that censorious politicians don't treat children's cancer research the same way, but in America they do. And maybe there's something to that connection: people addicted to control and power will suffocate anything that could give hope, cultivate critical thinking, and encourage empathy.

I want to go back to Walther Benjamin (and you can't stop me): "This is the situation of politics which Fascism is rendering aesthetic" (20). It was true when Benjamin wrote it in 1935, and it's true now. The US government's Department of Homeland Security used an image from *Halo* captioned "DESTROY THE FLOOD JOIN.ICE.GOV," comparing immigrants to the series' parasitic villain (Randall). More recently, Steve Downes, voice actor for *Halo*'s protagonist Master Chief, condemned the government co-opting his voice as propaganda for the illegal war in Iran (Downes). If you're wondering whether his respondents are overburdened with that critical thinking I mentioned, I can assure you they are not. Interestingly enough, none of the shills or bots I saw said the White House should keep politics out of games.

Complaining about politics in art ignores the fact that if artists don't get political, politicians will gladly manipulate art. One could argue, and many did on X did, so help me god, that it's OK for the US government to use *Halo* for military propaganda because it's a war game. And if humanity has to defend Earth against extraterrestrials, I'll agree. I'll even grab an assault rifle in the hopes that I'll get one of those cool alien guns. It's one thing to propagandize a sci-fi action game, but it is insane to use a game for children to dehumanize.

In September 2025, the Department of Homeland Security tweeted a video of ICE arrests intercut with footage from the Pokémon anime and mocked-up Pokémon-style cards of suspects (Moreau). It was all set to the Pokémon theme song which, honestly, is too good for people afraid to show their faces while arresting children. Nintendo, owners of Pokémon, are famously litigious, and I hoped they would treat this theft with the same kind of severity they treat "even the most innocuous [fan] projects" (Plunkett). Instead, the Pokémon Company said they didn't have anything to do with it. That's also all they did when the government propagandized *Pokémon Pokopia* (Yang) (Figure 6.1).

I can understand Nintendo not wanting to go up against the US government, but Nintendo doesn't mind suing the US government over tariffs (Zwiezen). The Pokémon Company said, "Our mission is to bring the world together, and that mission is not affiliated with any political viewpoint or agenda" (Yang). That is, unless that agenda is relatively easy to evaluate. Going after some copyright infringers and not others is a political choice, especially when the IP is being used for propaganda. A stance of neutrality fails upon contact with reality.

Games being "apolitical" doesn't prevent governments from stealing their assets to make propaganda any more than neutrality prevents politics from harming the games industry. This is why the games industry is finally unionizing: workers have no choice but to stand up for their rights because the government isn't going to do it. The Communications Workers of America organization has to struggle against government-approved media monopolies and police violating the First Amendment ("Campaign").

FIGURE 6.1 I'm still struggling to believe this is real. From the White House X account.

The 2026 Game Developers Conference, the "GDC Festival of Gaming," had 20,000 attendees, down from 30,000 the year before (Takahashi). This is in no small part to the trump administration illegally arresting whomever they like and incarcerating them indefinitely (Orland).

And this is over video games. All this strife and handwringing is over games. But they're important to us. Games can disrupt, disturb, comfort, and inspire because they are so immediate to their players. Walter Murch, Legendary film editor (and director of the nightmare fuel *Return to Oz*), put it this way while comparing movies to dreams:

> Along those lines, it is revealing that the words a parent uses to comfort a child frightened by a nightmare—"Don't worry, darling, it's only a dream"—are almost the same words used to comfort a child frightened by a film—"Don't worry, darling, it's only a movie." Frightening dreams and films have a similar power to overwhelm the defenses that are otherwise effective against equally frightening books, paintings, music. For instance, it is hard to imagine this phrase: "Don't worry, darling, it's only a painting."
>
> (*MURCH 30*)

For the record, this "power to overwhelm the defenses" is necessarily good. The ability of movies, games, and comics to punch through the proofing of our logical minds means they can more easily reach the most sublime or wretched chambers of our hearts. While our mental defenses sometimes prevent us from fully accessing the breadth of our emotions, they can also protect us from ingesting staggeringly stupid shit. Ethics and morality aside, what I've come to appreciate is that small and mean artwork is mostly tedious. Making better games isn't, and shouldn't, be about making our players better people. It certainly isn't going to make us better people. However, better art asserts that we are all people. The persuasiveness of that argument and the vivacity with which it is argued makes it true to the audience. No, better art doesn't make us better people, but it can remind us that we deserve to be, we must be, people who make a difference.

BIBLIOGRAPHY

Benjamin, Walter. "The Work of Art in the Age of Mechanical Reproduction." *Illuminations*, Hannah Arendt, Stocken Books, 1969, pp. 1–26.

"Campaign to Organize Digital Employees (Code-CWA)." Campaign to Organize Digital Employees (CODE-CWA), code-cwa.org/. Accessed 14 March 2026.

Downes, Steve. 8 March, 2026, https://x.com/SteveDownes117/status/2030736342464835675.

Moreau, Jordan. "Pokémon 'not Involved' with Homeland Security's Ice Raid Video Using Theme Song: 'Permission Was Not Granted.'" Variety, 24 Sept. 2025, variety.com/2025/digital/news/pokemon-homeland-security-ice-raid-video-not-involved-1236528305/.

Murch, Walter. *In the Blind of an Eye: A Perspective on Film Editing*. 2nd ed., Silman-James Press, Los Angeles, 2001.

Orland, Kyle. "'It Doesn't Feel Safe'-Many International Game Developers Plan to SKIP GDC in US." Ars Technica, 9 March 2026, arstechnica.com/gaming/2026/03/it-doesnt-feel-safe-many-international-game-developers-plan-to-skip-gdc-in-us/.

Plunkett, Luke. "Nintendo's Lawyers Need to Chill." Kotaku, 11 July 2025, kotaku.com/nintendos-lawyers-need-to-chill-1835858130.

Takahashi, Dean. "GDC Festival of Gaming Draws 20K Visitors, down from 30k Last Year." GamesBeat, gamesbeat.com/gdc-festival-of-gaming-draws-20k-visitors-down-from-30k-last-year/. Accessed 15 March 2026.

Randall, Harvey. "Microsoft Might Be Silent, but Halo's Co-Creator and Halo 2's Design Lead Have Called the US Government's 'destroy the Flood' Analogy Comparing Immigrants to Parasites 'Absolutely Abhorrent.'" PC Gamer, 29 Oct. 2025, www.pcgamer.com/gaming-industry/microsoft-might-be-silent-but-halos-co-creator-and-halo-2s-design-lead-have-called-the-us-governments-destroy-the-flood-analogy-comparing-immigrants-to-parasites-absolutely-abhorrent/.

Shafer, Ellise. "Wim Wenders Says 'We Have to Stay out of Politics' as Berlinale Jury Fields Questions about Israel and Palestine: Filmmakers 'Have to Do the Work of People, Not the Work of Politicians.'" Variety, 12 Feb. 2026, variety.com/2026/film/festivals/wim-wenders-berlinale-stay-out-of-politics-1236659726/.

Siegel, Alan. "Red, White, and Misused: How 'Born in the U.S.A.' Became an Anthem for Everything That It Wasn't." The Ringer, www.theringer.com/2024/06/04/music/born-in-the-usa-politicians-campaign-bruce-springsteen-misinterpreted. Accessed 9 Mar. 2026.

Wenders, Wim. *Wings of Desire*. Basis-Film-Verleih GmbH, 1979.

"Pokémon Rebukes White House's Use of Its IP in a Social Media Post." NBCNews.Com, 6 March 2026, www.nbcnews.com/pop-culture/pop-culture-news/pokemon-rebukes-white-houses-use-ip-social-media-post-rcna262057.

Index

Note: Page numbers followed by f refer to figures.

For Product Safety Concerns and Information please contact our EU representative GPSR@taylorandfrancis.com Taylor & Francis Verlag GmbH, Kaufingerstraße 24, 80331 München, Germany

Batch number: 10823811

Printed by Printforce, the Netherlands